PRACTICAL SOCIAL WORK

Series Editor: Jo Campling

BASW

Social work is at an important stage in its development. All professions must be responsive to changing social and economic conditions if they are to meet the needs of those they serve. This series focuses on sound practice and the specific contribution which social workers can make to the well-being of our society in the 1990s.

The British Association of Social Workers has always been conscious of its role in setting guidelines for practice and in seeking to raise professional standards. The conception of the Practical Social Work series arose from a survey of BASW members to discover where they, the practitioners in social work, felt there was the most need for new literature. The response was overwhelming and enthusiastic, and the result is a carefully planned, coherent series of books. The emphasis is firmly on practice, set in a theoretical framework. The books will inform, stimulate and promote discussion, thus adding to the further development of skills and high professional standards. All the authors are practitioners and teachers of social work, representing a wide variety of experience.

JO CAMPLING

PRACTICAL SOCIAL WORK

Series Editor: Jo Campling

BASW

Social Work with Old People

Second Edition

Mary Marshall

M

MACMILLAN

First edition 1983
Reprinted 1985
Second edition 1990
Reprinted 1990

Published by
THE MACMILLAN PRESS LTD
Houndmills, Basingstoke, Hampshire RG21 2XS
and London
Companies and representatives
throughout the world

Printed in Hong Kong

British Library Cataloguing in Publication Data
Marshall, Mary, *1945–*
Social work with old people.—2nd edn
1. Great Britain. Welfare work with old persons
I. Title
362.6'0941
ISBN 0–333–49497–0 (hardback)
ISBN 0–333–49498–9 (paperback)

Series Standing Order

If you would like to receive future titles in this series as they are published,
you can make use of our standing order facility. To place a standing order
please contact your bookseller or, in case of difficulty, write to us at the
address below with your name and address and the name of the series.
Please state with which title you wish to begin your standing order.
(If you live outside the United Kingdom we may not have the rights for your
area, in which case we will forward your order to the publisher concerned.)

Customer Services Department, Macmillan Distribution Ltd,
Houndmills, Basingstoke, Hampshire, RG21 2XS, England.

To all social workers who want to work with old people:
lang may yer lums reek.

Contents

vii

viii   *Contents*

Appendices   115

Preface

This book is a second edition and thus incorporates six more years of experience of working with older people. It is still no more than an attempt to share what I have learned over the years. Friends, colleagues, students and relatives will recognise themselves, their friends, colleagues, relatives and clients. I am grateful to them all. I am especially grateful to a small group of friends and colleagues who helped with this second edition and, in particular, my patient and skilful colleague, Evelyn Gibb, who did all the wordprocessing and prepared the text for publication.

Age Concern Scotland   MARY MARSHALL

Note: While the cases and examples referred to in this book are real, all the names used are fictitious and in some instances details have been altered.

1

What to Expect from this Book

This book is a primer. It is addressed to social workers who are beginning to work with old people and are wondering what social work has to offer. It is based on a conviction that we have a great deal to offer. Social work, as a new profession without the straitjacket of tradition, is ready and willing to adapt itself to new needs in society as they emerge. Britain's elderly population is a new phenomenon. Although it has been possible for decades to predict the ageing bulge in the population born at the turn of the century, nothing much has been done, and services are having to be adapted in a piecemeal fashion. Sadly this means that elderly people are seen as a 'problem' by most of the public services. An ageing population is not of course necessarily a problem. It can equally be viewed as a unique moment in history. For the first time the people who have made the history of the century are alive and able to tell us about it. Most children today will know elderly people, will know the rare comradeship that exists between the old and the young. Most adults will be able to hear about their families in the world wars or the Great Depression. The twentieth century has been one of extraordinary turbulence and social change, and we do not now have to rely on books, with their inevitable bias towards the educated and the articulate: we can actually ask people what, for example, it felt like to hear the first radio or what it was like to be in service. It is harder to get them to talk about the trenches; those still alive are determined on the whole to forget those terrible years. Nevertheless, unprecedented opportunities now exist to know the past.

1

For the first time also it is possible to look forward to perhaps twenty years of freedom in retirement to do those things that cannot be fitted into working lives. Opportunities are now being seized by older people, like the large numbers of older people doing Open University degrees. Working until you were incapable was the pattern until the second half of this century, and indeed losing work can be very traumatic. But for most people being old has its compensations, especially compared with the drudgery and deprivation of the interwar years.

So the 'problem' of the ageing population is not a problem for most people and need not be a problem for social workers. It can instead be an opportunity to work with an exceptionally interesting group of adults: those who have adapted to enormous change and coped with total upheaval of their lives, and who may need a little help to go on living the lives they, in the most part, enjoy and want to continue to enjoy. One of the real bonuses about offering a social work service to old people is that a little goes a long way. (This book will be full of rules of thumb; tested and tried but not substantiated by any research. More research on social work with old people is urgently required.) A little goes a long way is one of these rules of thumb that applies to all sorts of services, not just social work. Use of a chiropodist, for example, can make an old person able to walk, able to shop, able to eat enough, able to meet friends, able to cope and remain independent. But this little bit of help must be the *right* bit of help. There is no point in providing a raised lavatory seat when the problem is loneliness, no point in group discussions when the problem is a blocked-up hearing aid, no point in providing a regular visitor when the problem is poor diet. And this leads to one of the real delights of working with old people. Apart from meeting all classes and types of people, social workers can also provide an extraordinary assortment of kinds of help. Social work becomes a very creative process. Rather than just operating a procedures manual, we need new solutions for new problems.

Now for another rule of thumb: social work with older people can never be done in isolation. Unlike work with children, when decisions are often taken without any other professionals being involved, this is quite impossible with older people: people like district nurses, GPs and home helps have to be consulted. This is one of the challenges of the job, however exasperating it can be.

So, given an optimistic picture of social work with old people and a conviction that they need and respond to skilled help, how can a book like this be organised? For the sake of simplification – and realising the flaws in being tidy – I propose to organise the book on the basis of yet another rule of thumb, which is that older people cope pretty well independently until they are about 75, when most of them will begin to feel some sort of deterioration in their finances, health, social life or whatever. So the first part of this book will be an attempt to justify this division, and to explain in what ways the 60–75 and 75-plus groups differ.

Another distinction this book will make is between *direct* and *indirect* help. This is an equally false division, but once again there are benefits in the separation in order to organise the material. The book will therefore separate face-to-face work from behind-the-scenes help. What is meant by direct help is that traditionally perceived as social work: counselling individuals and groups, organising services and negotiating with other agencies and professionals on behalf of particular people. All the time the social worker has particular people in mind. Indirect help, on the other hand, concerns groups of people with a common problem. To some extent all elderly people share a problem, which is coping with and combating the ageism that is such a fundamental characteristic of British society. However, at a somewhat more limited level there are of course many groups who share needs and problems, like those caring for yet older relatives, or those in institutions. And this is where the confusion between direct and indirect work arises. In order to simplify, I have for the most part put the work social workers do with carers, be they relatives, friends, neighbours, volunteers or whatever, into the indirect section. Sometimes this work is clearly related to a particular elderly person, so this decision may seem a curious one. My intention is that by doing this we might get a better idea of the strains that all carers suffer, rather than assuming that those of us who are paid for it are somehow immune.

Indirect work can be concerned with work like generating resources or influencing public opinion, tasks not generally perceived as social work. But I have an optimistic notion of social work as the supremely adaptable profession that will meet the needs that arise (or see that they are met) rather than imposing the services we know about, whether or not they meet the needs.

This book will not make any distinctions between different settings for social work. By this I do not mean that all settings are the same but rather that I consider it unhelpful to see them as totally different. Old people are the same whether we meet them in hospitals, their homes or in residential settings. Their needs are different only to a limited extent in these different places, and my feeling is that social workers are much too willing to allow settings to dictate the services provided. Thus I plan to use examples of social work with elderly people in all sorts of different places. Having said this, it seems the right moment to come clean about my approach to social work with older people and the assumptions that lie behind it.

I believe that ageism is rife in British society. I think that old people are discriminated against both publicly and privately. They have little power, little status and few resources. Insults like 'geriatric' are used to describe our worst enemies. Ageism is no different from racism or sexism, except that there is a curious double think about ageism. It is highly discriminatory and yet at the end of the day it will affect most of us. Only time will tell whether our values will alter to accommodate the fact of a new kind of Western society where most of us can expect to live until at least the age of 70.

My second assumption is the opposite of ageism. I believe that each old person has a contribution to make and that older people as a whole provide a richness to society. Without a balance of older people in the population our lives in the 1980s and 1990s would be intolerable.

And third, I am, obviously enough, committed to the provision of skilled social work help to the older members of our community: not just because I think they should get the same as the rest of the population or because they deserve it for having built our society for us, but because social work as I see it is well suited to the needs of older people. Our value position, for example, that places each individual at the centre of attention, makes social work perfectly suited to people who are often lumped together as useless. Social work's commitment to self-determination as an underlying principle should make us preserve the right of choice for people who, generally speaking, have so little choice. Skilled social work help is needed by old people and commitment is needed to ensure that they receive it.

A final point on style. Everybody referred to in this book whose sex is not clear is assumed to be female. This may be rather exasperating since it is different from the normal custom. The reality that a great majority of social workers and old people are women is the reason for this decision, and it avoids the clumsiness of compromises like 'him/her' or 's/he'.

2

Our Elderly Population – Two Groups Not One

Background information

The last decade has seen a proliferation of data about the elderly population. Everywhere in local authority papers, articles and research project reports the basic demographic trends were spelled out. I am therefore going to assume that the trends are familiar, and supply merely for revision one diagram from Anthea Tinker's invaluable resource book, *The Elderly in Modern Society* (2nd edn) (1984) (see Figure 2.1).

Figure 2.1 shows that the population of citizens over 60–65 has increased dramatically and is now levelling off, but that the proportion of people over 75 continues to rise until the end of the century. In more concrete terms it means that for a city like Liverpool, the number of people aged between 75–84 was 26,716 in 1987 and will be 27,090 in 2001, and of the over 85s there were 6,981 in 1987, and will be 10,170 in 2001: a 43.8 per cent increase in the older age group. This is a daunting prospect since services for this group are already stretched beyond endurance, with no sign at all of any matching increase in services.

However, what I want to focus on here is why our population shape has changed so fundamentally, because I think that if we know the reasons we can trample on a few myths and have some better arguments to deal with the ignorance and ageism in society. There are two good ways of learning about population trends this century: one is to look at the pattern of births and deaths over the last eighty years; and the

6

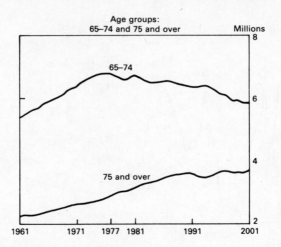

Figure 2.1 *Population projection for the elderly based on 1977 Social Trends*
Source: Central Statistical Office *Social Trends* (No. 9) London, HMSO,
1977, Chart 1.3.

other is to look at particular families. I want to do both, and to
start with a graph (Figure 2.2).

Figure 2.2 shows birth and death rates since 1900. The
twentieth century started with a high birth rate. Victorian
families were large, for example, Queen Victoria had nine
children, although she was an exception because all of her
children survived into adulthood whereas most families lost
some children on the way. Towards the end of the last
century, more and more children survived. The benefits of
sewage systems, inoculation against diseases, better diets and
cleaner water were beginning to show. So there was a population bulge at the turn of the century and these are the people
who are 80 and 90 today. It is misleading to say that people
are living longer only because of medical advances. It may be
true in that people do live an extra few years, but the huge
numbers of very old people are alive today because they
survived illness and infection when they were children. As a
country which pioneered public health measures Britain is
now reaping the dramatic rewards. Other countries which
followed will also have very large numbers of old people
within a couple of decades, while the Third World will prob-

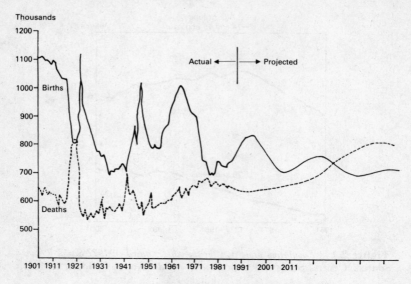

Figure 2.2 *Population changes and projections*
Sources: Graph adapted from Central Statistical Office, *Social Trends*
(No. 5) London, HMSO, 1974; and Office of Population Censuses and
Surveys *Population Projections 1985–2025*, London, HMSO, 1987.

ably see this same population bulge in thirty or forty years'
time.

In order to translate these bare facts into the experience of
one family I want to introduce the Monaghan family, whose
photograph is on page 9. This photograph was taken in 1915,
when, coincidentally, both sons were home from the army.
Here we have an illustration of the baby bulge of the turn of
the century, because no Monaghan children died in infancy.
This would have been unlikely a generation earlier. The
Monaghan family were reared in the centre of Glasgow and
were the beneficiaries of the improved living conditions, cleaner
water, etc., of this time.

Going back to Figure 2.2 it can be seen that the death rate
shot up between 1914 and 1919. Thousands were killed in the
trenches. There were, for example, 57,470 British casualties
on the first day of the Battle of the Somme. Thousands more
died in the influenza epidemic which swept Britain after the
war. The men who died left behind them countless widows

The Monaghan family

and women who would never find husbands. The Monaghans were incredibly lucky – both of their sons survived the war, though Jim was very severely injured as a sniper with the Royal Engineers. Mary, the oldest Monaghan child standing between her parents, lost her sweetheart in the trenches but was lucky enough to find another one.

There was also considerable emigration during these years. It can be safely assumed that the people leaving were more often men than women, and were almost certainly young people in search of work. (It is only just before and during the Second World War and briefly during the 1950s that immigration has involved a significant number of people.) In this respect the Monaghans are unusual. Only Ann, who stands to the right of her mother, left the country. She went to Australia, though she returned after several years. Many of the family left Glasgow, however, and scattered over the North West of England. This internal migration was considerable as younger people moved about in search of work during the Great Depression.

During the period following the First World War the birth rate dropped and stayed low right into the 1930s. Gone were

the big Victorian families, while large numbers of women had
no children at all. The Monaghans are typical in this respect.
Two daughters married, two did not and only one daughter
had any children: Mary, who had two. The sons all married
and had children, but none of the children had as many
offspring as their parents: the eight children produced only
sixteen grandchildren. The consequence of this dramatic and
prolonged drop in the birth rate can be seen today, where it is
exacerbated by the fact that after the age of 45 male mortality
rates exceed those of females. Today most men over 65 are
married (72.7 per cent), whereas only a third of women over
65 are married (37.5 per cent). Women are more likely to be
single (10.1 per cent to 7.3 per cent) and much more likely to
be widowed or divorced (52.4 per cent to 20.0 per cent).
According to Abrams (1978), 30 per cent of women had no
children, and 45 per cent had only one or two.

The elderly population in the 1980s is therefore a consequence of the history of the century. High birth rates at the
turn of the century, many male deaths in the First World War
and a low birth rate in the 1920s and 1930s provide an
explanation for the large numbers of old women who are now
on their own. The only surviving Monaghan children are two
sisters, one of them single and the other a childless widow.

It is important to understand what has happened in order
to have realistic expectations of, for example, family care.
How often do you hear the lament that families do not care for
old people like they used to? That sort of comment is based on
a failure to understand that families have never had such large
numbers of old people to care for. And that many old people
alive today simply do not have families. For social workers the
implications are obvious: we must treasure the family help
available, we must be considering alternatives to family care,
and we must not collude with the idea that there is some sort
of failure in the moral fabric of the nation.

The two groups

To make a dividing-line at 75 is a very arbitrary division. No
more arbitrary, of course, than suggesting that people are

automatically unfit for further work at 60 or 65. I hope that my reasons are more benign: I am making the distinction between the *young old* and the *old old* because I think it is helpful to social workers. Certain characteristics of each group create quite different sorts of problems for social workers to tackle, bearing in mind that social workers will only ever come into contact with a very tiny minority of old people. We must remember, however, that many older people in Britain were not born here or have lived much of their lives in institutions so do not share the characteristics of their peer group. Many elderly people originally from Asia and the West Indies, for example, have experienced great deprivations both in their countries of origin and in Britain. They can physically be much frailer than most indigenous British elderly people of their own age.

So what kinds of characteristics are different in the two groups? Let us start with the most interesting – sex. In the age group 60/65–74 there are 127 women to every 100 men. This is an uneasy balance of numbers, but nothing like as unequal as the over 75s who have 200 women to every 100 men. In the 85+ age group there are 327 women to every 100 men. What does this mean for the people themselves? We do not know. We only know that a lot of women in their 80s never had the opportunity to marry, or if they did it was only for a brief period. So some of them will have become accustomed to being on their own and will have carved out a life for themselves on their own. Indeed, they ran our schools, our residential establishments and our hospitals until fairly recently. Significantly they did not run our businesses or our parliament, and they were clearly accustomed to having men about who maintained a major role. How does it feel to be over 75 and without a man among your friends or in your home? It might be a tremendous relief or a major tragedy. Whatever the case – it will be different for each elderly woman – it is something that social workers should be aware of. I have, not surprisingly, concentrated on the predicament of women, but what about the men so severely outnumbered by women? Do they miss the comradeship of other men? Do they feel overwhelmed or delighted? There are no answers really, but it must be a curious feature of one's social life.

Linked to sex is the difference in family life. In the older group born around the turn of the century are the widows and single women of the First World War. As we have already seen, many of these women often do not have families. But it is important to see how this relates to age: the older you are, the less likely you are to be living with a family. In the age group 65–74, 17 per cent of men and 39 per cent of women live alone. In the age group 75-plus, 26 per cent of men and a staggering 58 per cent of women live alone.

Now for income, a topic not yet touched upon. Once again the consequences of ageing fall hardest on the oldest. The older you are, the more likely you are to be poor. Very elderly people are more likely to have used up savings, worn out their clothes and furniture and to be living on income support. This is particularly important given that older people have a greater need for warmth, better food and special help like particular kinds of aids, etc.

Two aspects of accommodation need to be mentioned. First, the older you are, the more likely you are to live in older accommodation. Many old people have grown old in one house, and have often been too short of money to maintain it in a reasonable condition. Older accommodation is more likely to be without basic amenities like inside toilets, insulation and hot water. At the same time the older you are, the more likely you are to be in some sort of institutional care, though the numbers are very small overall. About three and a half per cent of people aged over 60/65 are in hospitals or in residential care. This figure breaks down into about 1.4 per cent in the 60/65–74 age group and 19.2 per cent in the 75-plus group.

Health also deteriorates with age, though this is by no means inevitable. Audrey Hunt (1978) found in her study of old people at home that 98.9 per cent of the age group 65–69 went out regularly, whereas only 79.4 per cent of the 85-plus group did. Arthritis and rheumatism are the main complaints of old age and lead to reductions in mobility for large numbers, and these get worse with age. Mental ill-health is also a feature of increasing age for small numbers of people. Dementia is relatively more common in the older group. It is estimated that about 1 in 10 people aged 65 or more suffer severe, moderate or mild dementia. In the 80+ group the figure rises to something like 1 in 4. Sadly the highest suicide rates are found amongst old people, in particular those aged between 75 and 84: 332 in every million, as compared with the national rate of 85 per million.

Jobs and hobbies will be much more common in the young group than the older group. The reasons are quite obvious and I shall not spell them out, but the fact is important when considering the quality of life of the older group.

People who are in their 90s today were born in the nineteenth century. I have been repeatedly reminded by them that they have lived through three wars, not just two; many of them remember the Boer War and have memories of things like 'kruger soothers', which were sweets they bought as children. They were in their teens and 20s during the First World War, and watched their families destroyed around them. Vera Brittain's *Testament of Youth* (1933) and *Testament of Experience* (1957) take us through the history of this century from her point of view. She lost all the men most dear to her in the First World War. Those who had families were rearing them in the 1920s and 1930s and many of them retired in the 1950s and 1960s, some of them having seen their children die in the Second World War as they had previously lost their brothers and fathers. The years since the war have been relatively tranquil, and yet the pace of social and technological change can make life very baffling.

People who are in their 60s and 70s, on the other hand, were born around the time of the First World War and some were children during the Great Depression. Many of them bitterly remember the years without work and the hardships their families suffered with the means-testing and the poverty. They were the bulk of the fighting force in the Second World War, where men and women fought together and the war involved civilians as well as the armed forces. It is therefore their experience of this century that also divides the two groups in our older population.

In summary, then, it is useful to divide an old population into two only as long as it helps towards an understanding of the lives they lead and have led. Generally speaking, a person over 75 will have a greater chance of being female, alone, poor, badly housed and in poor health than a person under 75. But this is only generally speaking, and there are vast numbers of exceptions. Poignantly, it is the experience of many social workers that all these disadvantages often seem to affect one person, whereas other people suffer few of them.

3

Social Work with the Young Old

Retirement

Why should it be so insulting to people in their 60s to be considered old? Being referred to as old is derogatory and will be until some real consciousness-raising is done among older people themselves, or until retired people are paid enough to enjoy themselves. Once they are 'proud to be old' the label will cease to matter and I would not feel even faintly guilty about including people between 60 and 75 in a book about social work and old people. For the purposes of this book I will grit my teeth and proceed with society's definition of old, and include all those over retirement age. Does social work have anything to offer this group? To a large extent the answer must be that we offer much the same as we do to people in their 40s and 50s, since this group may well be parents of adolescents or have marital problems or be in hospital with normal illnesses of adulthood. But this group have their own particular hurdle to overcome: retirement.

Retirement is one of the most important of life's milestones in Western industrial societies. Its significance is overwhelming for all who have been reared to see their usefulness in terms of occupation. Work also provides social interaction and for many people who have retired this is what they miss most. It also provides a scaffolding for people's lives and a place for them in society. Social work with the unemployed is being acknowledged as important, and many of the problems of the retired are the same as those of the unemployed and thus

15

better discussed elsewhere. But social workers need to understand the significance of retirement if we are to help those who
seem to be going through an acute crisis. In socio-economic
terms retirement is a curious phenomenon. Most people's
incomes drop dramatically on retirement. Why have we not
established a reasonable income system for retirement? Chris
Phillipson (1982) argues that retirement policies are delib-
erately flexible and retirement itself is kept financially unat-
tractive in order to sustain a pool of reserve labour that can
easily be made available if the need arises. The truth of this
hypothesis may be tested in the next decade as the numbers of
young people entering the workforce drops.

The actual experience of retirement is for many people a
loss; a massive change in a person's life. Like any other loss it
must be made sense of before a person can move forward. It
seems likely that people who prepare for retirement cope
better with it. But most pre-retirement education is too little,
too late. Given that money and health are the main indicators
of life satisfaction in retirement, planning for retirement
should take place much earlier than it does. Mid-life planning
courses are emerging but for the 10 per cent or so people who
experience pre-retirement education it tends to be a week or
two around the time of retirement. Courses are often far too
formal, the participants being seldom able to influence the
agenda. Ideally courses should be highly participatory and in
a situation (unlike the workplace) where the group can continue to give each other support after retirement. However,
many people are very anxious prior to retirement, so perhaps
a course helps them feel better. Most people adjust to retirement perhaps because they have prepared for it. Just as
important as preparation is the extent of the loss. For some
people their job is the centre of their world, whereas for others
it is simply one of many activities they enjoy. Social workers
will tend to meet those for whom retirement was very difficult,
like Miss Leach, who had been the backbone of the workshop
of a small printing firm for nearly fifty years. This was a very
low paid job, but she could easily do every process involved.
She had lived with her parents, who had died many years
before. Now finally retired at 70 she had no social skills at all.
She was depressed and completely isolated from her street in

spite of the fact that she had lived there all her life. She had no idea how to make friends and she was leading a desperately lonely life. Regular visits from a social worker, superficially social calls, very slowly built up her confidence. She was very ill at ease at first, but learned how to chat, and initially timid contacts with her neighbours developed into reciprocity as she minded their houses for them or looked after their pets.

For some people redundancy or illness brings retirement very suddenly. It is in the latter group that social workers can be on hand to help make some sense of the experience. When I was doing research on old people in hospital I was much struck by the degree of despair of men in their early 60s who were realising that their illness would bring their working life to an abrupt end. These men were seldom referred to social workers since they usually had devoted families and they tended not to ask for help. They were often unwilling to worry their families, and badly needed a skilful stranger with whom they could unravel their complex worries about money, family problems and their futures. Our research was about discharge from hospital – a major focus of much hospital social work – but their problems were not in this area, and as such they were not problems easily recognised by the hospital. It would need a social work department with a real understanding of the extent of the loss in sudden retirement to recognise the unmet need for sensitive counselling in this group.

Loss of hopes and plans for the future are some of the most painful losses we all have to bear at some time or another. With sudden retirement can go the loss of all sorts of plans such as a last trip to Canada to see the grandchildren, or for a recently retired wife, enjoying being at home on her own all day for the first time for many years and hoping to have a couple of years peace. Talking through this loss of plans can clarify all kinds of hidden feelings and can ease the adjustment of all parties.

Everybody knows about the husband who is at home all day getting under his wife's feet, and causing tensions to emerge in their marriage. Many marriages thrive on periods apart, and retirement, particularly if it goes with illness, can force people together and place great strains on a relationship. Work also gives people something to talk about, and without it whole new patterns of interacting have to be learned. What can the social worker offer? Understanding first, of the surprise and hurt of experiences like unexpected marital problems, and some positive ideas about how skills and energies can be put to good use.

Making a contribution

The newly retired are the people who run our voluntary agencies, our church groups and advice centres. For many people the chance to directly help others is one of the pleasures of retirement. There are also vast numbers of jobs behind the scenes for those disinclined to be face-to-face with people with problems.

The Age Concern Edinburgh Advice, Information and Counselling Service, for example, provides retired people with the opportunity to make a very valuable contribution. At minimum they commit themselves to a period of apprenticeship, half a day per week in the office and monthly training sessions. Intensive counselling is provided by a special group as is a home visiting service. Volunteers can opt for as big a time commitment as they wish. Hundreds of older people and their relatives appreciate this service. One of the advisors is Mr Parker who retired from a major Scottish firm. He enjoys doing a useful job one morning per week. He also likes the fact that he can be flexible with the timing of his sessions to allow for holidays and other domestic commitments. He is not looking for the intensive personal contact of participating in the visiting scheme. Most of the volunteers in this service are people of retirement age.

It is in pointing the newly retired towards an activity in which they can feel useful and needed that social workers are so well placed. We know, or should know, about the various places where volunteers can be used both within our own departments and agencies and elsewhere. We ought also to be able to use our skills of assessing and matching so that people fit somewhere quickly rather than trail about offering themselves and getting increasingly discouraged.

There is vast literature on the use of volunteers so I do not intend any sort of resumé, but I do want to emphasise one or two points. There is a tendency to assess a potential volunteer in terms of the qualities they have that are most similar to ours. We social workers tend to evaluate the volunteers' ability to empathise, to listen, etc. If we are to point people in directions where they can find a useful niche for themselves, we have got to be more imaginative. There must be a job somewhere for every volunteer, says the Community Service Volunteers Organisation, and although I would not go all the way with that I do think that there are some wasted skills. Mr and Mrs Waterson were teachers and they decided to retire at the same time. Having been very active indeed in their jobs and in pursuits associated with teaching they were dreading retirement. Neither of them wanted to join visiting schemes; they wanted some useful activity which would use their intellectual and organisational abilities, but one from which they could take long breaks for holidays and visiting their children without letting individuals down. They also wanted something quite different from teaching children. The Citizens' Advice Bureau and a scheme involving collecting drugs for the Third World proved absolutely right for each of them, and they are enjoying their retirement enormously.

There are huge numbers of organisational jobs in voluntary agencies, like keeping the books, organising collections of furniture, fund-raising and transporting people which do not require an ability to communicate at any depth. There are skills to be learned with the Red Cross and St John's. At the same time there are newly retired people without the knowledge or confidence to join in. There are also some agencies that unofficially discriminate against older volunteers and we may have to take issue with them. Too often people are told they are too old rather than given the real reason for rejection. This is really unhelpful to the older person who may simply need redirection to something more appropriate. Social workers have a role here which is really preventive.

Many social workers feel that volunteers are more trouble than they are worth, and it is true that they often need training and always need support and supervision. If we are talking about the newly retired I think we should reconsider, because they do have a particular quality to offer to older clients: they are much nearer to them in age and experience than most of us. They are more likely to have cared for an elderly relative themselves. Indeed, when I interviewed the eight newly retired people working on a boarding-out scheme for old people I found that they had all got home nursing skills acquired in caring for their elderly relatives. The newly retired already provide the bulk of voluntary care for old people: they run day centres, they run visiting schemes, and they are active in all kinds of schemes organising holidays, transporting disabled older people and providing entertainment. Many of them are thus able to find a routine and a social circle, two of the most important things that work provides.

Success in this business of pointing people in exactly the right direction so that they are rapidly assimilated into some voluntary effort without losing their nerve requires a knowledge by social workers about what is going on in communities. At the very least, we should know certain key people to telephone for advice and suggestions. The local Council for Voluntary Service (or Council for Social Service, as it is sometimes called) is always a good place to start, with its role of co-ordinating voluntary agencies. Some even run Volunteer Bureaux, so the matching job is done. It takes a degree of confidence to go along and offer help – and confidence is quickly lost by people who have lost the main activity in their lives. It can make all the difference if any appointment has been arranged, or they can go to a meeting with someone else, or if a social worker has given them something to read about the project.

Caring for older relatives

The newly retired are often the people who care for their older relatives. Many 90 year olds are cared for by children in their 60s and 70s. Sometimes this care imposes an incredible strain. The strain can be physical and help needs to be organised for jobs like bathing, dressing and bedmaking. Sometimes the strain is emotional. People can be trapped at home with a mentally or physically frail relative and they may need a sitting service or respite breaks when their relative goes into some sort of care. Sometimes it is a question of money, and often these people could have claimed extra financial help like attendance allowance had they known about it. Sometimes social workers can best offer support to the carer by being a shoulder to cry on, a role criticised by people who feel that it is often provided as a poor substitute for services and practical help. In the case of Mr Davis it was a service no one else was offering. Mr Davis was caring for his mother in her 80s who had severe dementia. She was physically very fit but her behaviour was bizarre. She would strip off her clothes in the street, would talk rubbish constantly, engaging any passer-by, and she had to be helped in all her daily activities. Mr Davis had always lived with his mother. He was devoted to her and was looking forward to a retirement when they could have more time together entertaining other people (she played the piano and he sang). He found the change in her almost intolerable, but he was determined to cope. He was referred by his GP to the social services department, and the social worker was able to provide certain practical aids (like taps that could not be switched on by her, and a nursery intercom in her bedroom). His sister came two afternoons a week to sit with her mother who could not be left alone. What Mr Davis wanted from the social worker was attention for his own feelings. He was enormously restored by an hour or so every fortnight talking to the social worker, while his sister was caring for his mother. He could share his anger, his sadness and his intense ambivalence about this troublesome stranger who was his mother.

Caring for the carers is about sustaining their care. Most people want to care for their relatives but give up from sheer exhaustion. This can be prevented if care for the carers is provided early enough and reliably. Caring systems are like Humpty Dumpty, once they break down they often cannot be put together again. But they can be kept on the wall. An important principle is that help is available when people want it, and not at the convenience of the hospital or social services department. Once relatives know that they can get help when they want it, they will often cease asking. They can even test the social worker, like Mrs Thomas who had been promised a hospital bed for her very sick elderly mother whenever she was desperate. The social worker had to work all day to find a bed following a frantic phone call from Mrs Thomas. Once it had been found, Mrs Thomas changed her mind, and did not bother the social worker again. *Certainty* seems to the key – if the carer knows help is available when needed or on a certain date, he or she can usually continue to cope.

In summary, what has the social worker to offer in the way of direct help for younger old people? First, a recognition that retirement can be a crisis, particularly if it is sudden or accompanied by illness. And as a consequence of this recognition, social workers should be able to provide counselling help. Sometimes people will need advice on organising their lives without work. Second, social workers are often involved in helping those people who care for older relatives. The needs of these older relatives will be covered later in the book. Here attention needs to be drawn to a wide range of financial, practical and emotional help that needs to be provided when it is needed – the right help at the right time is the way to nurture these fragile care networks. A fuller discussion on ways of helping carers, not just retired carers, will be found in Chapter 5.

Selling the skills of the newly retired

This section will cover indirect work with the young old, though I do not feel that there is much behind-the-scenes social work to do for a group of people perfectly capable of doing it for themselves. The newly retired can usually expect a good ten or fifteen years in which to do all the things they ever wanted to do. There are lots of groups of pensioners, for example, who have a merry time in Spain every winter. They go from October to April and live nearly as cheaply as they do at home. They have great fun dancing the nights away and strolling from one bar to the next during the day. This is not a life-style that suits everybody, and there is another large group of pensioners going to universities or doing Open University degrees. Many older people are keen to seek educational opportunities in their broadest sense once they have overcome the often negative experience they had of education when they were young. The newly retired are the backbone of every kind of voluntary organisation, from gardening clubs to charitable good works to friends of museums. They are a vital dynamic force in every activity outside the daily grind of work. This makes the sad complaint of feeling 'on the scrap heap' so incomprehensible. Far from being on the scrap heap, the newly retired can contribute in almost any way they like. What is needed is a two-pronged effort. Social workers need to sell the skills of the newly retired and to convince them that work is not the sole purpose of life.

Most people do not want a totally selfish life. They want to feel that there are some demands on them, to feel that somebody needs them. Many people have families and other commitments to meet these needs, but other people are keen to make themselves available to help others, and social workers can help to make sure that advantage is taken of this pool of helpers. The first thing to be done is to wage war against the ageist attitudes that exist among some of our colleagues who use volunteers. Far too often social workers are looking for volunteers who are simply unpaid versions of ourselves. We should instead be promoting the special skills of the newly retired – their maturity, balance and life experience. There seems to be a fear among social workers that older volunteers are more rigid and less willing to learn than young ones, which must be nonsense. There is no reason why older people should have more fixed attitudes than younger people. Admittedly, they will have had their attitudes shaped in a rather different world, but there is no evidence that they are any less willing to adapt and change than other people. The reality is probably that social workers feel less comfortable with older people. Unresolved attitudes to teachers, parents and other people get in the way when we have to work alongside older people, especially in the very subtle and difficult relationship of social worker and volunteer. Perhaps if these matters were brought out into the open at staff meetings, training sessions and planning meetings, the air might be cleared. The skills of the newly retired have to be sold, particulary to agencies and projects that are working with older people. The generation gap is just that much less, and an older volunteer is usually much more acceptable to a very old person than a schoolgirl or student.

If social workers are involved in actually setting up a

project to attract and make the best use of the newly retired, there are several points to be considered. The first is that many newly retired people lack confidence, partly due to the demoralising experience of retirement and partly because they may be unsure of how to deal with this new experience. Projects need to make special efforts to explain what is required and exactly how an approach can be made. Ideally, potential recruits should be made to feel that they are inspecting the project rather than being evaluated themselves. The way that training is sold to volunteers requires special care. Many elderly people have had poor experience of education and are put off by the term 'training'. Training needs to be highly participatory. It needs to build on existing skills to build up confidence and it has to be enjoyable.

It may be important to recognise that the newly retired can be very short of money. Fares and expenses should be covered and a contribution to a meal can be made without jeopardising social security entitlement. It is also important to bear in mind that this group often have family commitments, both towards children and parents. Voluntary work needs to be organised in such a way that people can opt out for a period and feel able to opt in again. And this brings me to my final point, that this is a group of people far too easy to exploit. They may be seen as having vast amounts of free time and energy, which may or may not be true. Far too often they are overloaded with work at the beginning when they are only too grateful for it, and then they have to leave in order to get any free time for themselves. This is of course true of any age group, but sometimes the newly retired can be very vulnerable.

Convincing people that there is something to life once they have stopped work is a subtle business that will vary from person to person. Equally a lot of other people need to be convinced that the newly retired have a great many skills to offer. One of the problems in both these efforts is that social workers themselves can sometimes doubt whether this is really true. Clearly we need to really believe that this group of people has a potential contribution to make. Time can be well spent thinking about the ages of many people who contribute most to society in terms of culture, voluntary effort and general good works. When people are obviously contributing to the quality of our lives, we forget to notice their age.

4

Face-to-Face Social Work with the Old Old

Skills in day-to-day work with very old people are currently being acquired at a great rate. None of the caring professions can completely escape the demands made by the rapidly increasing numbers of very old people and their families. However, the extent and quality of this help is very variable. Social work agencies, like most others, have failed to plan for the changing shape of the population, so agencies and services are being adapted in the midst of overwhelming demands on what little help is available.

In addition, the amount and kind of help given is very patchy over Britain as a whole. Many social work/social services departments have now got specialist teams who work with older people. Sometimes these are teams of fieldworkers, sometimes they are managerial, policy or advisory teams. Well over half of new referrals to departments are older people but they are seldom dealt with on first contact by a specialist worker unless their contact is with a specialist psychogeriatric or geriatric unit. When there is an intake system very rarely are elderly people referred to long-term teams, few departments have any policy statements about the nature of the social work service to be offered to older people. Voluntary agencies are equally diverse: very few offer a specialist social work service from the start. I am not here promoting the concept of specialist workers in statutory and voluntary agencies, but it does seem that some sort of positive discrimination is needed. Agencies which deal with very old people as simply another group of clients do not seem able to resist the pressure, both internal and external, to make children and families

25

a priority when sharing out available skills and services especially the skills of basic grade social work.

This lack of uniformity of services makes it very difficult to specify what direct skills with very old people should be, so I have decided not to try to be comprehensive, but rather to concentrate on the extra skills that can be required when working with very old people. This may give the impression that very old people tend to be different from the rest of the population. On the whole this is not true and most very old people cope perfectly well without the help of social workers. Nevertheless, there are people who have particular problems, often relating to illness and disability, and they require a high level of skilled and imaginative help. I hope that what follows will provide some ideas for social workers working with these people.

I begin with *communication* as the most important skill. *Assessment* follows logically as the next step, though sometimes situations are so fraught that this is missed out. The remaining three sections cover three other kinds of skills that can be needed: first, social work at *crisis* times; second, social work with people whose lives are very *constrained* by infirmity; and finally, social work when *practical* help is required.

Communication

I start with skills fundamental to social work – communication skills. In this section I want to look beyond communication of information. Social workers must be able to communicate about feelings – our own and those of our clients. With this very vulnerable client group, feelings are probably the most important thing to be shared.

One of the essential prerequisites of communication as a social worker is to start where the client is. It is the client's perception of reality that is of interest. A second is that we should never judge our clients. These two principles are well enshrined in the literature as fundamental to social work, but they are especially important with a group of people who are in so many ways different in life-style and experiences, from social workers and other client groups.

I believe that social workers can share the experience of

being very old, but that sometimes we need to have some extra skills to achieve this. For a start we need to realise that people over 75 have a set of attitudes towards seeking help and expressing the need for help that were learned in the Depression and have been tempered by their experiences since then.

Until the middle of this century seeking help was an expression of failure, and being unable to cope was punished. Fortunately, we can gain some understanding of this from reading the life stories of old people that have been tape-recorded. Thomas Morgan, for example, says in Thea Thompson's *Edwardian Childhoods* (1981):

It ain't so long ago – in between the wars – if you had a piano you went to see the Relieving Officer – you was told to get rid of it. If you had anything decent they'd tell you to pawn it or sell it. Not give it away but sell it, to make up money to keep yourself. They were very abrupt, very abrupt. They bullied you. Oh sometimes when I see them bullying my mother I used to cry and creep out of it.

George Hewins also vividly illustrates the stigma of poverty when he describes some children in the workhouse in his book *The Dillen: Memories of a Man of Stratford-upon-Avon* (1981):

The older kiddies starts to congregate. Who should I see but Hilda Rowe and Violet. They's had their hair chopped off, weared long holland pinnas with big red letters: STRATFORD-ON-AVON-WORKHOUSE. They did some sort o' drill, then they was marched in a straight line to the National school across the road. The babbies' screams and those red letters haunted me all day. If I weren't hearing the one I was seeing the other. When I got home I told the missus but she said: 'It's to distinguish them.' 'Oo from?' 'From kiddies oo's Dad's working! Ow would you like our George (their son) took for a pauper?' 'Teddy Rowe was working', I said, 'till e went to the Infirmary.' He'd got TB. They took you to the Infirmary to die. I was angry: 'There's no need for them red letters! The pauper kids is distinguished all right! You can spot em straight away – they's up against the wall watching the others play! They ain't playin – and when they marches out a-night the other kiddies is callin "Workhus brats!"'

"Workhus brats!" They's distinguished all right! If I ever catches our George callin like that . . .' I could see she didn't think the same as me. She was wrong, the Guardians was wrong, and all of us, letting it happen. Why was you punished for being poor? Why do they part husbands and wives in the workhus, mothers and kiddies, tell me that? Some sent one way, some t'other, according? It's cruel!

We can also listen to old people. It is very salutary to hear old ladies say with pride that they never had to ask for help in spite of suffering the most appalling hardship. They are often very proud of their thrift and self-denial in circumstances that people today would have found difficult to tolerate with such fortitude.

Unless our efforts to communicate are based on some understanding of the life histories of very old people, we will fail to understand their reticence and unwillingness to ask for help. We will also make all kinds of other mistakes. It is in some ways a cross-cultural problem. In much the same way that Amrit Wilson (1978) describes the misunderstandings that arise because most ordinary British people have no understanding of the lives and attitudes of Asian women, most younger social workers have little idea of the lives that shaped the attitudes of very old people, particularly of women. Some old working-class women, for example, can be suprising in their lack of strongly held opinions about any of the major social events that they have lived through, and will always say 'my father used to say . . .' or 'my husband used to say . . .' and they find it difficult to communicate with young social workers who have strong views and do not mind expressing them. Similarly, it is sometimes almost laughable to hear elderly women who have been in service talk with pride about the families they cleaned for – or, on the other side of the baize door old ladies who are baffled and upset by their grandchildren who have gone into 'trade'. I am not suggesting that social workers should be social historians with an intimate knowledge of Edwardian attitudes to class, poverty, etc. But I am suggesting that this generation had their values and attitudes shaped in very different times. For many of them the world of the 1980s and 1990s is an indifferent and hostile one. Social workers can trample unwittingly all over their finer feelings unless we proceed with caution and care. It is perfectly possible to see the world through their eyes, but they have to do the telling.

A related issue arises with the ageing members of immigrant families. Sometimes they arrive as relatives of established families, and sometimes they were the original immigrants and have grown old in Britain. Their values will have been shaped in quite different cultures. With groups like old Chinese, West Indian and Asian people we face a double culture barrier of age and ethnic background, and sometimes a third barrier of language makes communication yet more difficult. Even in people who have learned English, the stresses of old age can make them forget and understand only their own tongue. Mrs Cortez, in hospital for an abdominal operation, was an old Spanish lady in her 80s who had been in England since she was 19. The stress of an operation and the need to have a catheter had resulted in her reverting to the language of her childhood. She appeared quite unable to understand explanations in English. The kindly but busy nurses coped by shouting in English and by dealing with her as briskly as possible. They were aware of her unhappiness and bewilderment but quite unable to explain anything to her. Interpreter services are underdeveloped in Britain compared with other countries like Australia which recognise their multi-cultural society. Alison Norman (1985) considers that elderly settlers in Britain are in triple jeopardy because they are old, because of the physical conditions and hostility under which they live and because services are not accessible to them. Social workers must have a real understanding of this experience if we are to communicate effectively.

Often reticence is due not so much to unwillingness to ask for help but to a genuine confusion about what is going on. Who are these strangers in my house? Special attempts at explanation and reassurance are needed, as are shown here by a first interview with Miss Gwenda Jones. She was an 87-year-old Welsh woman who was referred to the social services department by her GP, who was treating her bronchitis and was worried about the risk of hypothermia. Miss Jones answered the door pale, drawn and baffled. She seemed willing to allow the social worker into her front room in which she had her bed. The social worker encouraged Miss Jones to get back into bed before explaining who she was and why she was calling. A mention of the GP seemed to satisfy Miss Jones, but she still seemed agitated. The social worker suggested that she might make Miss Jones a cup of tea – an offer that was gratefully accepted. The social worker made no attempt to fire questions at the old lady; instead she encouraged her to relax and talk about herself using the photographs around the room to start the conversation. In this way she learned that Miss Jones had come with her parents from North Wales to the city when she was 10 and she still had a great many relatives in North Wales. She was somewhat aloof from the street and her social contacts were mainly with the Welsh Church, which she had not been able to attend for some months. The significant aspects of this interview are the need to respond to the situation in ways unusual when compared with interviewing younger adults (we would not normally make tea in someone else's house), and the importance of reassuring Miss Jones about her own identity. The temperature of the rooms and Miss Jones' financial arrangements are issues that cannot be dealt with in question and answer form when an elderly person is frail and anxious.

Communicating with people with dementia can be difficult, but it is absolutely essential that we do it well if we are to find out their views and wishes. The BASW Guidelines which I had the pleasure of editing (Marshall, 1988) has a useful section on principles of communication with people with this disease. It stresses the importance of setting a warm, accepting and compassionate tone to the communication which can be aided by touch and appropriate body language.

Dementia is a progressive illness so communication skills have to adapt to the stage of the disease the elderly person is experiencing. In the early stages there is a lot of anger, anxiety and depression. People try and cover up their diminishing competence or even deny it. A lot of elderly people become needlessly fearful when they cannot remember things because they fear they are becoming demented. Sadly, we cannot provide ready access to memory clinics so we have to provide an accepting approach in which people can share their fears. It can be useful not to ask direct questions which cause extra anxiety when the answer is not readily forthcoming. Once the dementia is well established and progressing, the elderly person may not be able to recall our names and roles so we have to continually introduce this to the conversation. There are some good tips for people with failing memories such as highly visible key hooks, clocks which give the date as well as the time, photographs with names, clear timetables of what happens each day and, of course, diaries. Writing things down can be essential and is a technique too seldom used by social workers who visit without leaving cards to say who we are, what we plan to do and when we will visit again.

Elderly people whose recent memory is failing will be comforted by their continuing ability to remember the past. This underlines the importance of getting as much information as possible about their past experiences so that we can relate discussions of the present with the past. It can also help us to understand oblique references or strange communications.

People with dementia need a lot of mental stimulation to function at the highest possible level. Sometimes this can involve discussions of the past using old photographs or other clues. It is important that old people with dementia have as many clues in their environment as possible. A group of nurses on a psychogeriatric ward found their patients with dementia behaved a lot better eating in hotel restaurants than they did in the dining sections of the wards. This must have something to do with the extra information provided by the presence of table cloths, cutlery, waiters and waitresses, etc., as well as higher expectations.

Reality orientation can be used to set up a particular regime in an establishment or as a technique used regularly in small groups of residents. We found many of the methods used very useful in a weekly group run in a long-stay geriatric ward (Marshall and Newton, 1981). The main aim of the group was to provide an enjoyable couple of hours for the patients, but we were also keen to engage them in activities which enhanced their self-esteem. We found that 'props' are very useful indeed in interacting with the patients. We tried to engage all the senses. We particularly used touch by finding objects with interesting shape or texture. Smell, using paraffin, soap or coffee, was less successful but bringing in familiar kitchen objects, photographs and magazines stirred up old memories in our participants. Once we even took in a little dog, which was a great success. It is probably the close personal attention and intense interaction that are the essential ingredients of reality orientation approaches, but the techniques are a great help in giving structure and purpose.

There is considerable debate about whether or not to put people with dementia right when they mistake people or places. The BASW Guidelines share a sensible principle when they say: 'setting people right for the peace of mind of the carer is seldom justified.' The decision about whether or not to put people right must depend on the individual circumstances, the degree of agitation and the importance of the misunderstanding. Sometimes it is necessary to swallow inhibitions and join in, the importance of the interaction being, of course, in communicating with the person inside. A simple illustration is an exchange between Miss Yates, a proud and educated woman, and a social worker. Miss Yates was angrily shouting at the day room about the mess in the office – files all over the place. The nurses ignored her, though they were mildly amused at the imperious way she ordered them to put the files in the cabinet. A social worker, who was in fact visiting someone else, went over to Miss Yates and asked her what she wanted. The old lady explained with some exasperation that the files on the table in front of her should have been put into the cabinet. The social worker picked up the tray attached to Miss Yates' wheelchair, walked across the room and put it on the piano. Miss Yates thanked her for her help and relaxed.

A similar principle applies when there are phantom friends and relatives who have to be consulted or included. Sometimes we may need to say that Cousin Betty can come too, or that we will wait while the client discusses the matter with Eva in the kitchen. It is not difficult to do but it demands that social workers can act on their decision to start where the clients are and accept their perception of reality.

Communicating with people reared in other cultures who are suffering from dementia is a very complex business. It is very easy to cause even more confusion if we are not familiar with the old person's culture. Mrs Chan believed that the social worker had killed all her grandchildren. The social worker thought that providing Mrs Chan with photographs of the children would remind her that her grandchildren were alive. Mrs Chan's daughter explained that Mrs Chan would traditionally only have displayed photographs of people who were dead so photographs of the grandchildren would reinforce her worst fears. This incident underlines the importance of seeking help and advice from other people from the same culture wherever possible.

Non-verbal communication is something social workers often neglect as a purposeful set of skills with all frail old people. Mrs Clint, for example, was very disabled with arthritis and totally blind. She said very little to anybody and it was assumed in her old people's home that she was living in a world of her own a lot of the time. However, one of the residential staff made a point of holding Mrs Clint very tightly when talking to her. Mrs Clint began to relax in the embrace and to talk very quietly. It was clear to the residential worker that Mrs Clint was acutely anxious a lot of the time about what was going on – she was of course unable to see. She turned out to have a salty sense of humour and a shrewd survival philosophy. She became able to join in conversations as long as she had the anchor and reassurance of personal contact. This seems, in my experience, to be true of a lot of frail old people. They need the steadiness of a warm hand to enable them to relax and participate. Many, many old people must be 'touch hungry'. Who holds them, warms them and strokes them? This must account for the importance of pets for many old people. It always seems a shame that the need of babies to be nursed cannot be more often matched with the need of old people for physical contact. And there seems to be a taboo on touching one another. A social worker ran a most successful group in an old people's home. The group always started with the members sitting in a circle holding hands and wishing each other 'good morning'.

Sometimes old people have to communicate in very complicated non-verbal ways. I say 'have to' because in some instances what they want to say is hurtful or unpleasant. Social workers accept this in children when they use play as a means of understanding things that children cannot put into words. Family therapists, too, use sculpting, which lets families express feelings they cannot speak about. I was with a group of social workers recently who were trying to understand why an old lady suddenly began to fall. She never hurt herself, but she was falling several times a day and causing frantic consternation to her neighbour, her caretaker and her home help. It emerged that both the caretaker and the home help were going on holiday and that the neighbour, who was getting very fed up anyway, was going to be left with the total responsibility for this fragile old lady. How could the old lady say 'Don't leave me' when she had no claim on any of their attentions. She had probably guessed, too, that the neighbour was reaching the end of her tether. Interestingly, she was admitted to an old people's home and the falls stopped immediately. Non-verbal communication can be especially important to people with dementia. They need extra information from touch, stance and tone of voice to supplement verbal communication. They are sometimes unable to put their feelings into words and judgements have to be made on the basis of whether they behave as if they are relaxed and comfortable. Mr and Mrs McInnes live in a specialist nursing home for people with dementia. They believe their room is a caravan. They go to the 'shop' each day to collect their meals and are clearly very contented as they sit either side of the window chatting about the weather. They would be utterly baffled to be asked if they liked living in a nursing home.

Verbal communication can have a particular quality with the very old. For example, it is useful if social workers realise the significance of reminiscence. Old people reminisce to remind themselves of who they are. This is why they do it more when they feel their identity or their life is at risk. If social workers know an elderly person well enough, we can use the extent of reminiscence like a barometer. An old lady I once visited regularly talked incessantly about her childhood and early adulthood when she was frightened that she would have to give up her home and go into hospital, and again on the anniversary of her brother's death. A lot of feelings can be expressed in reminiscence which cannot be talked about in a more straightforward fashion. Tales of times that were particularly frightening or worrying can indicate current fears and worries. So apart from being interested in oral history social workers must be alert to feelings behind the stories. Why does Mrs X have to talk about her children? Is it because, like so many older women, her years as a young wife and mother were the most significant of her life, is it because she needs to reassure herself that she was once important to other people whereas at the moment she can see she is just a liability, or is it because it is comforting to recall a time when she felt in control of her destiny?

Social workers may baulk at the obvious implication of the above, i.e. that talking to elderly people may take a lot longer than talking to younger adults. Certainly it does seem to be true that a slower pace is necessary with very old people. But it must be true also that social workers try to move much too quickly with most clients: we drop in for ten minutes in passing in order to relay really crucial information about foster homes or court hearings. The one thing old people usually have is plenty of time, a major asset when it comes to offering time and attention to each other or to distraught daughters. But it can be irritating, given the way we social workers dash around balancing twenty different balls in the air at the same time. I sometimes think that the same could be said of social workers as is said of GPs: that if they took more than two and a half minutes per consultation, patients would not return again and again. If we organised our time to give older people more time, we might avoid the frustration so often felt at sitting listening to an old person when we should have been somewhere else half an hour before. The trap, of course, is that intervention is so often purposeless: a call is made to see that they are all right, and two hours later the social worker is bored out of her mind by a lonely old lady. If the help had been planned properly, we would have realised that merely dropping in on a lonely person is cruel when what they need is a proper amount of attention. Time should have been spent organising someone else to go. Being clear about why visits are made and what it is hoped to achieve must be the way to deal with the frustration and guilt that underlie so much social work with old people. Social workers cannot visit simply as friends. If we do, it must be in our own time.

Finally, in this section on communication I want to talk about one of the most delightful experiences I have had working with very old people, which is that, however confused, demented or disabled they are, singing can break down all the barriers to communication. I know well the pleasure of singing with groups of frail older people, sometimes holding hands, or catching an eye across a room. It is something everyone can do given familiar songs. Presumably our older citizens sang a great deal more in their youth than young people do today. They certainly remember the words and tunes of old songs. There is not nearly enough singing in old people's homes, hospitals and day centres. The quality of it is quite unimportant, but social workers must join in.

One of the underlying themes of this section has been a suggestion that social workers need to break out from the pattern of purely verbal exchanges with clients. We are dealing with people who are often emotionally or intellectually frail, who often have some sort of sensory loss and who are sometimes leading very insecure and unhappy lives. Social workers need to be very creative and uninhibited in ways of communication if we are going to share the feelings of our clients.

Assessment

Assessment is not something that ever stands on its own and the word should always be followed with 'For what?'. When frail old people are concerned it generally means assessing people at home for their eligibility for the services offered, and for the degree of risk they are coping with. Only too often the first becomes a routinised mental shopping list as social workers go through lists of services. This can even become a substitute for assessment of need. One hospital social work department I knew had assessment of need as their objective and yet each patient was classified as 'needs home help' or 'needs meals on wheels'. What they should have had of course was a list of needs like 'lonely, needs company', 'stiff, needs help in the house'; this might have led to more imaginative attempts to meet these needs than simply adding names to waiting-lists for local authority services. But this is a digression – I am assuming that social workers should be in the business of assessment in more sensitive terms than just doling out local authority services.

What I propose to discuss under this rather too general term of 'assessment' are the assessments of need and risk that are done by social workers when they first interview an elderly person at home. I feel strongly that social workers should be able to do a fairly comprehensive assessment at the initial stage in order to avoid a string of strangers calling on an elderly person to assess her in countless different ways. With a bit more trust it should be possible for a social worker's assessment to be adequate for a home help organiser, a health visitor and certainly for any other sort of social worker. But we must have a mental agenda in our minds. It is no good going in with a questionnaire: all you will get are the answers the old person thinks you want. The topic of interviewing elderly people has not been sufficiently researched, although there is some evidence that factors like whether they have been interviewed before and time of day are important.

So let us take an imaginary ideal interview. The social worker arrives late morning or mid-afternoon, never early in the morning or late in the afternoon. Ideally, the social worker has written to say why and when she is coming, but this is sometimes not possible. On the doorstep the social worker waits long enough for Mrs Brent to have a look at her through the sitting-room window and then to get to the door. It may be important for the unknown social worker to look tidy – I have often had elderly people say that it was because I looked reasonable and honest that they let me in. When Mrs Brent answers the door the social worker produces an identification card and explains who she is – a connection with a familiar person is always helpful – 'Dr Y suggested I call', or 'Your home help Mrs So-and-So asked me to visit'. Sometimes it is worth going in with a friendly neighbour, who may have been the person who asked the social worker to visit. Mrs Brent invites the social worker in and walks ahead down the passage. Social workers, in my opinion, do not use their eyes and noses often enough: we are trained to listen but a sharpening up of all the senses is invaluable. How does Mrs Brent walk?

What does she hold on to? Are there loose mats on the floor? What does the house smell like? Is it damp or cold? Having arrived and sat down, the social worker can be watching to see how easily Mrs Brent gets in and out of her chair, or whether she is wearing proper shoes. It is seldom difficult to get a conversation going as long as Mrs Brent can hear; if deafness is suspected, the social worker sits well in the light facing Mrs Brent. It often takes some time to calm an elderly person if the call is unexpected – discussion about the photographs is always a good starter. The interview should never proceed with a series of questions unless Mrs Brent is expecting this and can cope with it. Much more fruitful is a conversation about health, for example, often starting with the obvious: 'Your chest is not too good, is it, Mrs Brent?' Or the conversation can be about relations and visitors, starting from the photographs. It takes time, but if a proper and reasonably accurate picture is wanted, time is needed. I think an hour and a half is probably enough, but half an hour is worse than useless, and unless the elderly person is very sociable she is left behind baffled and anxious.

But back to the mental agenda: what is on it? Start with the basics – food and warmth, then health factors, the most important being mobility (feet, arthritis) but also the chest, heart, eyes and ears. What is needed is not a diagnostic label but some idea of the degree to which health factors are affecting independence, and what is being done about them. Then consider the activities of daily living, like bathing, dressing, shopping, cooking, and getting in and out of bed. And then the whole area of social functioning; the actual number of social contacts is less important than their perceived value, unless we are purely in the business of surveillance. And finally, look at the subtle issue of feelings. Has Mrs Brent suffered a bereavement recently? Does she feel that life is worth living, that she can get help in an emergency, that she wants to continue living at home?

A lot of this lengthy agenda can be answered by watching Mrs Brent and looking at her circumstances. Perhaps some of the stories she tells upset her and she looks very bleak. If social workers want to learn how to watch as well as to listen, a day spent with a GP is very useful. GPs assess skin colour, sparkle in the eye, obvious loss of weight and so on all the time, and much of their diagnosis is based on what they see rather than hear, particularly with older people, who too often assume that a cold, painful, worried existence is an inevitable part of growing older.

If Mrs Brent mentions a much beloved neighbour or vicar or lunch club it is often worth a visit, because the extent to which there is a problem will often be measured in a rapid change in circumstances in some way or another. Mrs Brent may have suddenly become confused or suddenly lost weight or suddenly lost her sparkle, and it is these sudden changes which should ring warning bells.

Above all social workers need to know what Mrs Brent is bothered about. She may be unable to climb the stairs to go to the lavatory and be quite happy to use a bucket, but she may have lost her nerve about something quite different, like her fear of falling when she bends to switch on the gas – or, sadly and increasingly commonly, she may not be switching on the heat at all because of the terrifying bill she received last time. Death may well come into the conversation. Many old people have got some savings to pay for the funeral. But sometimes this can be a cause of considerable concern, and social workers should be sure that we do not deflect this issue when it is raised because we dislike talking about it. It is often a topic that old people themselves do not like to discuss with their relatives, and a social worker might be most welcome if she can organise the will to be written or the funeral arrangements to be made. And sex can be something that old people feel inhibited about discussing with friends and relatives. Fears that someone has designs on them can be a great source of agitation, and yet are not things that old people feel easy discussing. Social workers must be seen to take these sometimes unlikely tales seriously, and we can be a great comfort to the old people.

To summarise this section on a general assessment of an old person at risk: be comprehensive, do not interrogate, seek second opinions and be ready to deal with sometimes rather surprising or shocking sources of anxiety.

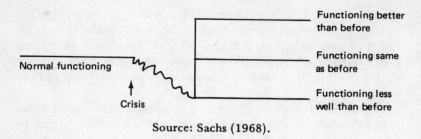

Source: Sachs (1968).

Figure 4.1

Crises

Many social work agencies are only able to provide a crisis service for very old people. The decision is not one I propose to comment on – rather to offer some suggestions on how to work with crises. Even in agencies offering a wider kind of service a crisis is often the reason for the first social work contact. Perhaps a swift revision of *Crisis intervention theory* would be useful. Writers like Parad (1966), Caplan (1964) and Rapoport (1962) have, in their different ways, suggested that people are particularly receptive to help when in the midst of a crisis, and that if a crisis is coped with it can even have advantages since the person will be more confident and able to cope better subsequently. Definitions of crisis vary but the general principle can be expressed diagrammatically (see Figure 4.1).

People hit a crisis where their normal coping behaviour fails to resolve a problem and they collapse helplessly. Recovery can be to a higher level, the same level or a lower level than before. It is during the collapsed phase that social workers are often involved. It is important that social workers understand certain principles of helping at this stage:

1. Some events are known frequently to result in a crisis for a person, but a crisis is not the event; it is the state of personal distress. Crises must therefore be defined by the sufferer and not by the situation.
2. People are very vulnerable and may be persuaded to take decisions they will subsequently regret.

3. Practical help is important to minimise extra worries.
4. Being there and staying calm may be all that is possible, but it can provide considerable support.

The literature on bereavement, such as Carole Smith's *Social Work with the Dying and Bereaved* (1982), is very useful here. Colin Murray Parkes' classic text on bereavement (1975) describes several stages to bereavement which include alarm, searching, mitigation, anger and guilt. Although these stages may not always follow each other in sequence, they are often present, and realising what is going on can make social workers panic less and offer helpful reassurance. Peter Marris (1974), in *Loss and Change*, builds on to his studies of bereavement and suggests that you cannot move on to the new until you have made some sense of the old. For all these writers a crisis or loss can be an opportunity to achieve a new identity.

One aspect of crises that is not discussed by the theorists is the question 'Whose crisis?'. It is generally assumed that it is the sick old lady or the bereaved old gentleman that is having the crisis (although of course theorists like Parad make it plain that what is a crisis for some people is not for others). Social workers need always to ask the question 'Whose crisis is this?'. It is usually the client's but quite often it is the social worker's: overwhelmed and exhausted on a Friday afternoon when suddenly confronted with what looks like a need to do a section before going home. Sometimes it is the agency's; as one cynic suggested at a course I taught: 'A crisis is when the social services department has no official procedure.' We have seen social work agencies go to pieces when attacked by the press or subjected to sudden, unexpected cuts. If the sufferer were identified more accurately every time, I am sure that theoretical knowledge of crisis theory could be applied to solving the right problems.

However, on the whole social workers see elderly people and their families in states of crisis. For the rest of this section I want to look at a number of events that are known to be common causes of personal crises in old people and their families. Some comment will be made on the kinds of behaviour that may occur and some suggestions made on how familiar principles of crisis intervention can be used in efforts to help. The events I want to consider are bereavement, loss of a home, discharge from hospital, admission to care and compulsory removal from home under sections of the National Assistance Act 1948 and the mental health legislation.

The death of a close relative is an experience with which old people will be more familiar than the rest of us. Little is known about bereavement in older people, though there seems to be an assumption that many of them have learned to cope with this particular loss. It is not safe to proceed on this assumption given the current state of knowledge – it is more useful to consider that the absence of overt signs of bereavement may simply mean that they are expressed in some other way like hypochondria, illness, listlessness or confusion. It is worth remembering a lesson well learned with younger people but seldom applied to the older: life decisions should not be made soon after a bereavement. As far as possible decisions like whether or not to go into long-term residential care or to move in with a daughter should be deferred. People with memory problems because of dementia may need the social worker to be the 'keeper of the memory' who reminds them when they forget that someone has died.

An unrecognised crisis seen much more often by housing managers than social workers is the result of a temporary or permanent loss of a home. For most of us our lives are bound up with a whole lot of possessions and particular places. Even when it is a welcome move to a new place there are inevitable losses. Mrs Dane, for example, was moving to another city with her daughter who had changed her job. The new house was going to be smaller and more convenient, but for the three weeks or so before the move Mrs Dane became increasingly confused. She recalled how every inch of the house had memories, many associated with her dead husband. The social worker was able to reassure the daughter that this was probably a painful crisis for Mrs Dane, and that the confusion would probably fade once she was settled. This turned out to be the case.

This temporary confusion is a familiar phenomenon in hospital wards, sheltered accommodation schemes and old people's homes. All the normal principles apply, and social workers need to understand what is going on and explain it to the staff involved. They need to make sure that there are not practical problems – like feeding the budgie – that are exacerbating the crisis. And they need to stand by offering calm and support plus reassurance – if it is true – that all will be well. Many crises are a consequence of loss, which must be made sense of before the future can be faced with equanimity.

Discharge from hospital is slightly different and can be a particular cause of crisis in its own right. Discharge from the all-embracing security of hospital to the fragile networks of community care can be a very traumatic experience. It is a very important part of the work of hospital based social workers. It is a real tragedy for old people that hospital social work has borne such a high proportion of cuts in many authorities. Getting all the right services to arrive at the right time is an organisational feat of the first order, and one which often fails. With community services provided by so many different agencies, all with their own criteria for eligibility, it is not surprising that things go wrong so often. What is surprising is that this particular crisis is given so little coordinated effort by health and social services. I can almost hear the hackles of the hospital based social worker rise – and of course coordinated care on discharge is often organised impeccably on geriatric units. However most old people do not go into geriatric units – over 50 per cent of all hospital beds (excluding maternity) are occupied by those over retirement age. It tends to be the run of the mill surgical, orthopaedic and medical beds that fail to give enough attention to planning the discharge of their elderly patients. The skills required by the social workers are as much concerned with influencing professionals as actually providing a service to particular patients, and will therefore be discussed in Chapter 5. At this stage perhaps it would be helpful to note useful skills to help particular patients. One is to be sure that the right questions are asked and recorded (one list of useful questions is shown in Appendix I). Another is to be sure that the patient is interviewed soon enough: it is no good waiting for a discharge date before interviewing a patient if it takes two weeks to organise a new electric fire in the bedroom. Another is to have a really good information system, and this is discussed in due course. It need not, of course, be the sole responsibility of the social worker. Burley *et al.* (1979) describe the impact of the geriatric team model on an acute medical ward. A consultant in geriatric medicine was attached to acute medical wards. All new elderly patients were seen if they presented complex problems and full assessment made by the social worker. The occupational therapist and physiotherapist were involved where it was relevant. Patients were then reviewed regularly at a case conference. The mean stay for all women aged over 65 was reduced from 25 to 16 days and for women aged over 85 from 50 to 19 days. The proportion staying under two weeks was significantly increased. The authors attribute their success to a number of factors which include obtaining a prompt and complete social report.

When people are very anxious they sometimes tell lies when interviewed. When discharge arrangements are being checked old people might say that there are people at home to care when this is simply not true. Similarly, many elderly people will underplay their ailments if they think that they will be considered unfit to manage any longer in their own homes. Others may feel that the hospital wants to get rid of them, that they are a burden to the ward. In my experience of interviewing hundreds of old people about their plans on discharge, only a very tiny minority have misled me. And it has always seemed to me to be their right to do so. However, an important principle is illustrated, namely the extent to which elderly people feel that they are victims and not masters of their own fate. This feeling can, of course, be an accurate assessment of the situation. Mrs Topliss, for example, was told she had to vacate her hospital bed within two weeks. The doctor told her and her nephew that he had done all he could and that Mrs Topliss needed nursing care in a nursing home. There being no social worker on this ward, Mrs Topliss' nephew spent all his evenings and weekends finding a nursing home into which his aunt was moved just within the two weeks. She was never consulted and being very dependent on her nephew, felt unable to voice an opinion. We should always be sure that we have convinced elderly patients that they will make the decisions and we will do our best to comply.

And now back to one of the most painful situations that

social workers are involved in – the decision to go into long-term residential or nursing home care. How can the gloomy picture of hasty decisions, uneasy social workers, distressed old people and unsupported residential and nursing home staff be improved? This final staging-post on life's journey is often approached with dread by social workers and old people alike, the residential and nursing home workers ignored like the old person once the deal is done. Perhaps the best way of dealing briefly with this process (which needs a whole book rather than a section in a chapter) is to look at an ideal admission.

Mrs Brent, living alone in a crumbling terraced house in the inner city, has been frequently hospitalised with pneumonia, a broken femur and a mild heart attack, all in the last eighteen months. She is increasingly forgetful and will not spend any money on heating. Meals on wheels and a home help are provided and neighbours keep an eye on her. At 89 she is the only one of her contemporaries still living in the street. She has no relatives nearby, a niece lives in another town with a family of her own. Mrs Brent has been thinking about residential care and her niece as well as the social worker have discussed it with her. The picture is a complex one for people in this position in relation to both what to expect from a home and all the different agencies and people who provide them. In relation to the first there are some sensible books available such as Rosemary Bland's *Is It For Me?* (1987) which goes through the concerns most often expressed by older people like Mrs Brent. This will equip her to consider what issues are important to her such as smoking, sharing a room, visiting arrangements. At this stage discussion in a small group of people in Mrs Brent's position can be very useful. Running a group is more thoroughly covered later in this chapter. This group, or indeed Mrs Brent, could visit several places to meet the residents and discuss the pros and cons so that she has thought through the whole business without pressure.

We now assume that Mrs Brent has finally agreed that she must go into residential care. A place becomes available at 'The Limes', and the sequence of events is as follows:

1. The social worker who knows Mrs Brent goes to 'The Limes' to talk to the officer in charge about Mrs Brent, and then goes to see her to initiate discussions about a potential move.

2. The social worker knows that Mrs Brent is very attached to her home help and to the family next door, so they are included in the discussion.

3. The residential worker goes with the social worker to see Mrs Brent some days later to talk about 'The Limes' and to offer Mrs Brent an opportunity to go and have a look.

4. Mrs Brent and the home help arrive at 'The Limes' for the day. The same residential worker is on duty and makes sure that Mrs Brent is given a cup of tea and shown round.

5. Mrs Brent is given plenty of time to make up her mind, and offers of further visits are made and accepted.

6. The social worker checks that Mrs Brent knows she can go on a trial basis at first, so although arrangements are made about her furniture the actual date of relinquishing the tenancy is not decided. The social worker also checks that 'The Limes' will take Mrs Brent's favourite chair and collection of ornaments.

7. A date of departure is decided well ahead, giving time for farewell rituals. The social worker photographs Mrs Brent in her house and at her door.

8. The social worker transports Mrs Brent to 'The Limes', where the residential worker is ready to greet her with tea (or sherry). Another resident has agreed to look after Mrs Brent. The social worker agrees to visit soon, and makes sure that the home help and neighbours will also be able to visit.

9. After six weeks a meeting is held with the residential worker, Mrs Brent and the social worker. Does Mrs Brent want to stay at 'The Limes'? Would she like to sign an agreement to stay, and another to authorise the clearing and selling of her house?

This list of events of the simplest kind of admission illustrates some important principles, which are no different from any long-term placement of a child. Time is given to making the decision and then making the move. Familiar people are always around to help with practical problems and to offer support. No final decision is made until everyone is convinced it will work. And there are important rituals associated with departing from one life and entering another.

The reality is of course usually very different. Sometimes it is easier because the elderly person has been a day visitor for some months and knows an old people's home. Sometimes it is more difficult because the old person is confused or sick. Usually admissions are done in a hurry when a carer falls ill or a hospital bed is urgently required. It is the emergency admission that makes nonsense of proper social work practice. Most local authorities now have systems for admissions to their own establishments that treat emergency admissions as temporary so that normal procedures of assessment and review can take place. These days it is admissions to the private sector that can be far too hasty. The private sector combines the very best as well as the very worst so this is by no means generally true. Many private homes use the very best practice in pre-admission, admission and review procedures. However there can be unseemly haste. Some private proprietors are motivated by an ill thought out motive to 'rescue' old people, others by the financial losses incurred by empty beds. The lack of control by any agency over admissions leave it open to bad practice. Sadly colleagues such as hospital consultants can be responsible for hasty admissions as can relatives who often dash in for the crisis and think they have sorted everything out by admission to a home. Mr Jerome for example was extremely frail and vulnerable, facing the possibility of living alone for the first time after over sixty years of marriage following the death of his wife. His daughter stayed behind after the funeral and arranged for her father to go into a nursing home where he died five weeks later. Neighbours, friends and other relatives stood by helpless and felt torn with guilt afterwards because they had not been able to help him die in his home as had his wife.

Emergency admissions are in my opinion to be avoided at all costs – and this actually happens in some authorities, where a battery of short-term help, like peripatetic 'daughters', moves in to sustain home care until the crisis is past. Often the crisis does pass. With a short-term respite, and some counselling a daughter can recover from a bereavement, or a holiday might restore the health of an exhausted spouse. But social workers are going to have to polish up on skills of resource generation, being tough with fellow professionals and securing the backing of colleagues. The thing about admissions to long-term residential and nursing home care is that they solve everybody's immediate problems at a stroke – except usually those of an unhappy old lady. We have to be ready to stand alongside her and incur the wrath of neighbours, relatives, GPs and consultants if necessary.

Finally, in this section on crises I want to look at the very rare occasions when a *compulsory admission* is considered. The legal aspects of the Mental Health Act 1983, Mental Health (Scotland) Act 1984, Mental Health (Northern Ireland) Order 1986 and Section 47 of the National Assistance Act 1948 (for England, Wales and Scotland) as far as compulsory admissions are concerned are described in Appendices III, IV, V and VI. Guardianship provisions are now included in all the mental health legislation as a way of providing protection and support to mentally disordered people living in the community. This protection and support is limited to determining place of residence and ensuring attendance for treatment. It includes ensuring attendance for occupation, education or training. Guardianship has been a controversial procedure because it has been used to remove reluctant old people from home or to compel them to attend for day care when they may not wish to do so. However as many people with dementia are in fact admitted to residential care or hospital against their will or without informed consent, then it can be argued that the use of guardianship affords a better safeguard of their legal rights.

I want here to look at the problems presented by compulsory admissions and some of the skills that can be appropriate. Compulsory admissions under any legislation are a very drastic sort of intervention in that they deprive people of their liberty. They can be a response to a crisis and they can cause a crisis for the client and for the social worker. There is nearly always the question of whose needs are being met and the consequent guilt when the needs of somebody else are put ahead of those of the elderly person.

A response to a crisis can sometimes be an overreaction, particularly when social workers are tired and drained of energy. The tendency to panic is far greater when people around us are in a panic too. Mrs Beatty lived with her mentally handicapped son. He was in his 50s and she was in her 80s. She had fallen on her way back from the lavatory and lay behind her bedroom door. Her son was making cups of tea for her and together they passed several days not seeking help in case it meant admission to care for both of them. Finally, a neighbour called and was dismayed by the smell and general chaos. She rushed round to the GP, who in turn rushed round to the house and insisted that he wanted both of them out of the house right away. He telephoned the social services and the duty officer came immediately. Mrs Beatty absolutely refused to go into hospital. In the ensuing panic Section 47 of the 1948 Act seemed the only answer. Fortunately, this tale has a happy ending since Section 47 requires that an establishment agrees to admit and in this case a geriatrician visited. He had the skill and confidence to examine Mrs Beatty on the floor, to get her into her own bed and to establish that she had not broken anything but was very severely anaemic.

Let us look at the skills of this geriatrician. He was able to see through the stench and the chaos to a very anxious and undernourished woman. He took time to reassure her and to talk to her. He knew that many alternatives were possible before compulsory admission was considered: intensive district nursing, day hospital assessment and a neighbour who might provide a hot meal. He recognised the 'trial by media' phenomenon in the degree of panic and anxiety in the GP and social worker, both feeling that they would be penalised if Mrs Beatty died in these circumstances. Confidence, time and knowledge are all needed and could equally have been shown by the social worker. Why should the social worker have panicked? Probably because the GP was really putting the pressure on her. Probably because she knew almost nothing about old people. Probably because she was really frightened that Mrs Beatty was going to die and that she would be in trouble for not having 'done something'. Keeping a cool head in these circumstances is very difficult, especially if there are a lot of other very pressing problems to deal with back at the office. And we share, along with most British people in modern society, a tendency to overreact to dirt and smell. Two mistakes often made are, first, to assume that the responsibility is all the social worker's, and second, to assume that old and frail people are incapable of making rational decisions about their lives. Mrs Beatty knew why she was refusing admission and had very good reasons. She would have responded well to a bowl of soup and a blanket wrapped around her while the social worker consulted all concerned.

Case conferences, whether impromptu or carefully organised, are a means by which social workers can share responsibility rather than taking it all on to our shoulders. They work rather like snow shoes – if you spread the load, you are less likely to fall into the snowdrift. Responsibility should be shared with GPs, community nurses, neighbours, relatives and anyone else involved. Social workers should never feel that a problem is theirs alone. In my opinion compulsory admission should never take place without a case conference agreeing to it and recording that agreement. Sadly we social workers work too often on our own. We sometimes do not get the appropriate support from colleagues, let alone other professionals. Looking after ourselves in these stressful circumstances is one of the topics covered in Chapter 5.

The use of Section 47 is an issue that should not pass without comment. BASW policy is that this section should not be used at all, and indeed it is not in many parts of Britain. I hope that this is because in these areas there are enough resources to keep people at home, but of course it is possible that some other sort of coercion is used instead. Alison Norman examines Section 47 in detail in her excellent book *Rights and Risk* (1987). I want here simply to give my own opinion, which is that this is an ageist piece of legislation which lacks clarity and proper safeguards. It should not be used except in those very rare cases when someone is too physically ill to make a rational decision, and when there is a strong likelihood that the admission will make them recover.

It seems to me that there is no justification for using it for people who are going to die. Studies like that of Forster and Tiplady (1980) have shown that most people removed from home under this section die quite soon afterwards, and this seems inexcusable. It should also never be used as an easier alternative to public health measures or to mental health legislation. At the moment there does seem to be a real drive to improve both English and Scottish legislation for older people at risk. Age Concern England have produced the excellent book *The Law and Vulnerable Elderly People* (1986) and Scottish Action on Dementia has produced *Dementia and the Law: the Challenge Ahead* (1988). Both books made very useful suggestions about new legislation. The point is that legislation should empower social workers to insist on arrangements that assist the old person remain at home as comfortably and safely as possible as well as to remove them from home only when absolutely necessary.

Social workers are committed to self-determination, and if people want to live and die in squalor, then whenever possible it should be our duty to let them. There may be a struggle to achieve this but it is to be hoped that this kind of decision will be shared with all the professionals involved.

Mrs Jack was referred to the psychogeriatrician who visited with a social worker. The GP was demanding psychiatric admission. The distressed home help organiser was putting pressure on the social worker because Mrs Jack would not let a home help into the house. A visiting health visitor thought 'something should be done' so she was pressurising the GP. The psychogeriatrician and the social worker found Mrs Jack in a squalid house surrounded by heaps of dirty tin cans and dishes, piles of newspapers and a lot of general confusion and mess. They decided she was not mentally ill (though exhibiting every sign of what is known as 'Diogenes Syndrome'). Since she did not want admission or any other help they left her.

Mrs McKelvie was similarly living in great filth and mess when she was visited by a worker from a Care and Repair project who offered to obtain repairs and improvements on her flat. Mrs McKelvie accepted this help with enthusiasm explaining that she had resisted all the other professionals because they wanted to put her into care. She was decanted into another flat while her own flat was cleared and refurbished. She is quite delighted by the change and is now a much more cheerful person.

The mental health legislation is somewhat different in that most sections have to be signed by two doctors and they have to provide a bed. However, a general atmosphere of crisis and confusion often surrounds this sort of compulsory admission. Mr Turner lived on his own, and in a modest and unexciting way he coped well with his limited mobility and low income. He had lived all his life in his parents' house, and was known by his neighbours without having any close friends. Suddenly he became very paranoid. He began hammering on the wall of his house, claiming that rays were coming out of the television into his brain. He began to deteriorate in physical condition and rather too often he had his flies undone. He kept telephoning his sister claiming that a particular neighbour was out to kill him. Finally, one of the neighbours called in a social worker, who realised that the sudden deterioration in this man of 79 was a sign of mental illness (which turned out to be paraphrenia, an acute schizophrenia in old age that often responds to treatment). Mr Turner was unwilling to go into hospital for psychiatric treatment so the GP and the social worker arranged a section. This was done and he returned home six weeks later after successful treatment.

For elderly people who have been periodically suffering from psychiatric illness for many years it seems that the process of sectioning them is much the same as if they were younger. Conversely there are people with dementia in long-term wards who persistently ask to go home. There is a big question about whether they need to be sectioned since they are clearly held against their will.

It is mentally ill old people without psychiatric histories who elicit mixed feelings and often a section is avoided or only done after much postponement and unnecessary suffering all round. Why should this happen? One reason may be a difference of opinion about whether some sections of the mental health legislation are appropriately applied to people with dementia alone. The implication of compulsory admission is that treatment is possible and this may not be the case.

There is a major underlying problem, which is the difficulty of separating the mental and physical components of illness in old people. A depressed old person, for example, may turn out to have pernicious anaemia, or a person in acute pain may appear to be severely confused. In terms of treatment old people often need both medical and psychiatric attention. Yet our services demand that they be labelled one or the other. They can end up being passed between the two services like a hot brick, or alternatively they can fall between them. Difficulties can, of course, be overcome if the services see collaboration as a priority. The Royal College of Psychiatrists and the British Geriatric Society are well aware of this problem, and in a joint policy statement called *Guidelines for Collaboration between Geriatric Physicians and Psychiatrists in the Care of the Elderly* (1978) they have written:

(i) Responsibility should be determined by the assessed needs of the patient, and not by quirks of referral. For example, if a patient with a gross motor stroke is referred to a psychiatrist, he is no less the responsibility of the medical services through having first made contact with the psychiatrist; and vice versa with a patient with severe depression.

(ii) Lack of resources does not alter the definition of responsibility. Once a patient's needs are recognised as falling within the province of one service, that service should support the patient within the limits of the feasible – even if this is less than ideal; a 'psychiatric' patient does not become 'geriatric' simply because there are no psychiatric beds, or vice versa.

(iii) Despite the foregoing there are patients who fall in a 'grey' area where they might appropriately be dealt with by either service. This then becomes a matter of negotiation between the two services, but the service which first made contact retains responsibility until ultimate placement is agreed. Patients must never be allowed to 'fall between the two stools'.

(iv) The principle that responsibility is determined by the patient's needs applies equally to patients admitted under compulsory orders. A patient admitted under the Mental Health Act may occasionally need direct admission to a medical (or surgical) bed, and a patient admitted under the National Assistance Act to a psychiatric bed. The belief that an elderly patient who is admitted under compulsion will necessarily be disruptive or insist on leaving is understandable but mistaken. There is rarely difficulty with such patients in general wards.

This is easier said than done, of course, given the general lack of resources, but perhaps social workers could use documents like this more forcefully. A common rule of thumb is that if the person can stand up they are psychogeriatric and if they cannot they are geriatric. This may sound heartless but the need is for treatment, and making patients someone's responsibility is half the battle.

Shortage of beds exacerbates the situation. Old people are supposed to stay longer in hospital than younger patients. The fact that this is often appallingly true is a function of ignorance about the care and rehabilitation of old people. A good psychogeriatric service does not need a lot of beds but it takes a lot of skill and effort to keep mentally ill old people at home. Some people shelter behind the excuse of a lack of resources. There is a general lack of knowledge about the psychiatry of old age. Very few GPs or psychiatrists will have had any special training in this field, and most social workers will have had none at all. However, there is increasing interest in dementia which is only just in time given the explosion in numbers of older people with this disease. BASW has produced *Guidelines for Social Workers Working with People with Dementia and their Carers* (Marshall, 1988) which provides information about dementia and presents some issues and skills for social workers. A consequence of the lack of knowledge – besides general muddle and haphazard treatment – is a significant lack of therapeutic optimism. Old people are not seen as people with mental illness but as people who have permanently and irretrievably damaged brains. While this may be true for some, many old people can be helped by correct psychiatric treatment, and some can be cured. Depression, for example, is often misinterpreted as dementia and appropriate treatment is not provided.

To revert to the theme of crisis, these situations are crises for friends, neighbours and professionals, if not for the old person concerned. Social workers can see all the symptoms of a crisis in people's behaviour: previously learned behaviour is just not adequate to cope with the circumstances. They can behave in a frantic way which often seems childish. They are usually very emotional and upset. Social workers move in and we have it in our power to solve the problem by organising the removal of the source of the problem. Sometimes we may be in a state of crisis ourselves. But simply removing the person is a very short-term solution. Feelings of anger and guilt linger on for years. I met a woman at a conference recently where I was speaking about the trap carers find themselves in. She said she had put her mother in a home twenty years ago and she still felt guilty. This feeling of guilt is very likely to be quite inappropriate but it is nevertheless very painful. Compulsory admissions should be as planned and purposeful as anything we do. We need to take time to share the responsibility and to see the admission as part of a sequence of care rather than an end in itself. In this way 'loss' can be given some meaning for everyone concerned.

The fact that we are talking about compulsory admissions near the end of people's lives should not preclude this need to make plans. Sadly there is usually a whiff of ageism in the air and compulsory admission is done with a lack of concern for the future that would never happen with young people. Finally, if powers of compulsory admission have to be used, there is a great deal that can be done to minimise the crisis for the old person concerned. The experience can be made more bearable by surrounding the old person with familiar faces, by explaining what is being done, by explaining their rights and making sure they know them, and by sharing plans for the future when the current crisis has passed.

In this section on crisis intervention we have looked at several different potential causes of crises. There are ways that social workers can help in crises by understanding the dynamics, by providing competent practical help and by being prepared to stand by offering support and reassurance. Social workers are also involved in hasty admissions to old people's homes and nursing homes and in doing sections. These situations should be avoided, but if they arise every effort should be made to treat the old people with exactly the same regard as if they were 25-year-old relatives.

Constrained lives

At the other extreme from crisis intervention there is a small group of old people suffering from chronic illness or disability who are highly dependent on others: relatives, nurses, care assistance. They suffer often from boredom, frustration, help-lessness and despair. Social workers do relatively little direct work with this group, though we are often involved with relatives. On the whole we tend to spend our time organising others to care by setting up day care, volunteers, clubs, etc. This is undoubtedly appropriate but there is something to be said for having some skills in helping this group, if for no other reason than to be able to understand the predicament of carers and to offer them the right sort of help. The communi-cations section at the start of this chapter considered some skills of communication with disabled people, so here I shall focus on the institutional settings in which many severely ill or disabled old people pass their time: in the lounges of day centres and old people's homes, in day wards of long-stay hospitals and day centres and day hospitals.

People whose lives are very constrained by illness and infirmity can easily lose their identity as people, since the preoccupation of those around them is to make sure they are physically cared for. Thus in long-stay wards and establish-ments the staff concentrate on making sure that the old people are clean, fed and toiletted. Often this is all they have time for, but the danger is that they will lost sight of the personalities in their care, and routine physical care will become of overriding importance. Social workers can do little to help in actually washing, dressing or feeding. They can, however, spend time responding to old people at an emotional and intellectual level. This can be difficult – not just because the old people cannot always see or hear or speak properly, which I have mentioned before – but because of the extra problem imposed by their location. For a start some institutional settings are poorly run and the elderly people smell, have food spilt on their clothing, and often look dirty and unkempt. Sometimes the physical disability itself gives them a frightening appear-ance. There is considerable skill required in concentrating on personality in such circumstances – the skill lies in ignoring their appearance or in accepting it as a fact without letting it put you off. Miss Jackson, for example, was vastly overweight. She lived in an old people's home with a very overworked staff who spent their time caring for residents with severe mental and physical problems. Miss Jackson had thin, wispy hair and an immense bulk. She was possibly constipated; whatever the cause she was clearly slightly incontinent of urine. Food was spattered over her whiskery chin. It took some stamina for the social worker to engage the wise sardonic humour of Miss Jackson and to discover that she was frightened that she was going mad, like so many other of the other residents.

A more common problem of relating to individuals in these crowded settings is that of privacy. Sometimes it is impossible to take the elderly person to another lounge or bedroom. There are some tips, however. The first is to be sure to get on the same level – never converse standing up when the client is sitting down. There is a risk of varicose veins if you squat, so the best idea is always to get hold of a chair or stool. It is always worth doing this even if the staff feel you are making a bit of a performance about it. You may have to insist given that chairs round the edge of the lounge are often jammed very close together and apparently spare chairs may 'belong' strictly to one of the residents. Kneeling is not good, again because it cannot be done for long enough, and suddenly standing up can disrupt the conversation. Another tip is to hold on to the person you are talking to. Even a light touch, on the hand, may be enough; it sustains contact and adds intimacy to the interaction. Avoid questions. Start by stating facts and leading outwards. Thus it would be better to say 'it has been a lovely day today' than 'Isn't the weather nice?' because the chances are that they will not have noticed and will feel very much at a loss. People in institutions are often experts at 'small talk' and it is often necessary to engage in a vast quantity of it before moving on to the main subject. And finally, use their proper names a great deal. There is nothing like the use of a name to enhance a feeling of individual worth in settings where christian names are often used much too freely, or 'love' and 'ducks' are used instead.

One way social workers can make a very useful contribution to the quality of life in residential settings is in running a group. This has the advantage of being very easy to control in terms of the amount of time taken, though the time factor must not be underestimated since it may need a lot of preparatory work. Another rule of thumb is that the success of a group can be measured in time spent planning. It is important to be sure that the social worker's objectives are congruent with those of the agency. If less than five out of ten incongruence is scored, then probably someone else in another agency needs to be asked to run the group instead. Thus a group of relatives caring for demented old people would be highly congruent in aims if these were to help them maintain the care of the old people, but highly incongruent if the aims were to teach them how to force statutory agencies to relieve them of the care of the old people. This may seem a far-fetched example, but I am constantly astonished by the kinds of groups social workers expect our agencies to allow us to run. So first select the aims, and then make sure that they are as far as possible congruent with those of the agency. Then consider a list of practical problems like location, time of day, activities, funds, numbers of leaders, open or closed, time (limited or not), membership and rules. If each of these is thoroughly worked out, endless miserable reappraisal is avoided. As far as possible it is sensible to elicit the involvement of any senior and any closely related staff in this planning process. For example, the matron of the old people's home will then understand why a lounge is needed for the group alone, or a ward sister will negotiate with the cleaners if 'messy' activities, e.g. like arts and crafts, are planned.

It would probably be helpful to look more closely at the suggestions above, assuming, for illustration, that the plan is for a group in an old people's home. First, decide on the aims. Are they likely to be acceptable to the agency? How can the aims be explained to the staff as well as the residents? Without the cooperation of the former, any group in a residential establishment can be instantly sabotaged. Staff will say that Mrs So-and-So is ill, or that she and her fellow residents do not feel up to it today. What are the chances of success? Sometimes it is worth reducing the grandeur of the aims and envisaging a series of small steps rather than a large leap. Thus it might be decided to give the residents a pleasant two-hour diversion with opportunities for conversation, rather than a fully fledged discussion group which they and the staff might initially find threatening. The next problem is location. Where can a group like this be held? Obviously a lounge is ideal, but does this mean turning out the other residents? Sometimes it is better to have a more unfamiliar place so that group time is different and special. All participants might sit round a table in the dining room in the early afternoon (a good time in residential establishments, as long as you leave at least an hour after lunch for a quiet doze). Activities depend on aims and membership. I once made the stupid mistake of trying to organise a discussion group, not realising that there was a very high incidence of deafness on the ward at the time and that a lot of hearing aids were not functioning. Activities must be matched to aims and must be adaptable. Thus making soft toys is ideal if the aim is to enhance self-esteem because the most incompetent can tack together two squares, and the most proficient can make toy lambs (see Newton, 1979). Mixed activity groups are often appropriate to keep people's attention. Thus a combination of exercises, craft work and singing might be a good mix. Funds are always required, so where does the money come from? Some planning groups get very bogged down on this point. In my experience charitable money can be forthcoming in small amounts for this kind of venture, so I would always start with the local Council for Voluntary Service (CVS). Leadership must be thoroughly sorted out. Some groups need two leaders – too many is confusing for old people if they are to relate in any qualitative way – but two allows one person to be in charge with the other participating, which can be helpful in groups which need a lot of encouragement. And it is always helpful to have two people for planning sessions. Open groups are easiest in residential establishments, but closed groups are a more significant experience: participants feel that they have joined something special. In my opinion all groups should be time-limited. Ten to twelve sessions sustain commitment and make sure that progress is reviewed even if the decision might then be to do another sequence, or to turn the group into a club type of occasion. Membership criteria depend on the aims. People who are very confused can gain a lot from singing and simple ball games, but they will not participate easily in discussion. And finally, rules – all groups have to have them. Imagining how to deal with certain types of problems is one way to formulate these. What can be done if people lash out with their Zimmers (walking-frames), or if they go to sleep, or if they fail to attend?

I hope this simple list of planning considerations illustrates how a well-planned group rolls along, in sharp contrast to the vexations of learning as you go. There is an ever-increasing volume of sensible British group-work literature which is easy to read and very helpful indeed (e.g. Preston-Shoot, 1987). Very little of it is about group work with the very old, but it all applies. Finally, without wanting to demean old people at all, I can recommend toddler playgroup materials as useful bases for activities with mentally frail very old people. The large simple toys provide opportunities for achievement as well as activities to discuss, simple games give an opportunity for aggression and humour, pictures can be talked about or cut up or made into collages for display. Of course, singing is always a pleasure.

Practical help

Practical help is often denigrated as 'not really social work', as if it were so simple that anyone could do it. This is simply not true, as we prove daily by not doing it very well. Practical help is what people often need from social workers, and, given willingly and to the best of our ability, gains us respect and appreciation from clients. This is shown in *Means and Ends in Social Work* by Goldberg and Warburton (1979), who investigated a district office and its clientele. Clients, it transpires, do not expect social workers to be successful and know only too well how hard it is, but they do appreciate us when we try.

So what are the components of effective practical help? They are: first, to get the information correctly from the client; second, to have correct and up-to-date information about available services; and third, to be able to match these effectively. Actually providing practical help in the sense of scrubbing floors or painting rooms is probably a poor use of expensive social work time. There are exceptions, however: social workers who shrug their shoulders helplessly when confronted with a cold old lady and a dead coal fire earn little respect from anybody. Sometimes quite disgusting jobs have to be done for fragile old people who trust no one else. Mr Goldrein, for example, was a musician and a composer who had vast piles of sheetmusic all over his filthy flat. It was quite clear that he had never thrown anything away, and amidst all the piles of music were little caches of old tins, potato peelings and rubbish. He would allow nobody to clear up the place and was languishing in hospital, too fragile to go home to such a degree of mess. He did, however, trust the social worker, who finally persuaded him that she would sort through his flat and at least make the kitchen and bedroom habitable. Sadly, the consequence of using the 'dirty squad' of the public health department is that they sometimes remove everything so that the place is clean but the old person has lost treasured, if rather grubby, possessions.

These occasions of actually scrubbing and mending are rare, and practical help usual means organising services of some kind. But first it is important to be sure that we know what is required. There is a fine and skilful line between accepting the presenting problem as *the* problem, and leaving people an opportunity to say something else if they want to. Often, of course, people need practical and emotional help, but equally often the attention is focused on one or the other when both need skilled and careful consideration. Most new clients have one big emotional hurdle to overcome which is asking for and accepting help from strangers. People in the early stages of dementia, for example, with failing memories and increasing bewilderment, find asking for help extremely difficult often because they are preoccupied with denial or with concealing their problem.

Mrs Carey illustrates the balance of practical and emotional problems in someone who has come to terms with asking for help. She came to a district office about a telephone. Allowing time to let her talk about her circumstances showed the social worker that she was very run down, agitated and depressed. If transpired that her husband had died after a long illness during which she had nursed him night and day. She was now alone in a ground-floor flat and fearful of everything. She had lost touch with her few friends because she had spent all her time with her husband, and she was clearly not eating very well. Having poured all this out, Mrs Carey was able to see that she was neglecting herself in every way. She agreed to try and see more of her friends and to eat more. The social worker warned her that bereaved people often fall ill themselves, and agreed to fill in the telephone application form, while warning Mrs Carey that she would not even hear whether the application had been successful for six months. She ascertained that Mrs Carey was not interested in rehousing, and gave Mrs Carey her card in case she wished to return. Correctly identifying problems is a skilled job, as social workers know from dealing with anybody who asks for help. Incidentally, Mrs Carey illustrates the important principle of trying to establish a shared contract. The social worker was quite open about what she saw as the problem, which was the bereavement rather than the telephone. Mrs Carey could have rejected this, but at least she knew exactly where she stood.

Social workers usually store their information in an impossibly disorganised fashion, demonstrating the low priority given to a service which is so highly valued by clients. We store information mostly in our heads, an unreliable system that works only if we give ourselves proper time for recall, and means that if we are not there nobody can share our expertise. Some information we store in filing cabinets. These bulge with things like out-of-date lists of day centres which no one ever has time to organise. If we have a notice-board we pin random pieces of paper which slowly curl up and go brown as they go out of date. We usually have somewhere a small and battered telephone book with everything in it. No one but ourselves can decipher the crossings-out, the cross-references to other pages or the peculiar system we have for putting certain numbers under certain headings. Some crucial bits of paper are poking out from under the blotter or the filing basket, some vital lists are in our top drawer. So, for instance, when Mrs Carey asks for the name of a solicitor who does free sessions at the local community centre so that she can sort out her will, we scramble through the filing cabinet, comb the notice-board, search our phone-number books, yell across the office to a colleague who has a brain like a telephone directory (to discover she is out), and finally have to resort to telephoning the community centre to discover that the service is now provided by the Citizens Advice Bureau on Tuesday evenings at six. This has probably been announced at a staff meeting but nobody wrote it down.

So what is the answer to this stressful and wasteful process?

First to give information the priority it requires. Information is one of the main tools of the trade and it needs time, thought and effort. Computers are the ideal tool but they are usually used for client records rather than information storage. After much practice I have ended up considering that there is only one really efficient low tech. way to store information, and that is on a *card index*. Use the big cards with the lug for classifying purposes and the smaller ones for the information. The secret is to classify according to the service provided and not according to the agency. This has the extra advantage of being an *aide-memoire*. Thus the bigger cards have things on the lug like SHOPPING, VISITING, NURSING AIDS, HOUSING, and the smaller cards have all the different agencies who supply shopping or visiting or nursing aids. Thus some agencies are on several cards, but there can always be a cross-reference like '*see Age Concern – shopping*', if the details of Age Concern are under the VISITING section. In my experience the small cards need the following information: name of agency, address, telephone number, person to speak to, services provided, criteria for eligibility, other important information (see Figure 4.2).

The advantages of a box filing system are considerable, the most important being the ease with which the cards are updated once it becomes a habit. Merely write a fresh card and throw the old one away. Other advantages are that they are a reminder of what is available, they are accessible to colleagues, and they do not curl up and go brown. The only danger is that you become an office resource because of your impeccable information and you never get a moment's peace!

Some sorts of information are clearly not amenable to simple classification since they require considerable knowledge. DSS Benefits are firmly in this category. Every social worker should invest in the annual publication *Your Rights* produced by Age Concern. We should also be prepared to talk through with older people some of the resistance they have to claiming benefits. The resistance can be because they see it as begging or they resent invasions of their privacy and independence. Information alone is seldom enough for older people: they need to see how it applies to them. Attendance allowance is one of the benefits least well claimed by older people. They

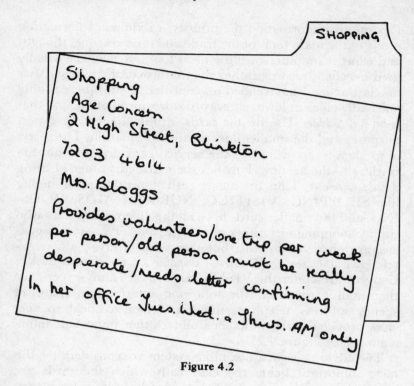

SHOPPING

Shopping
Age Concern
2 High Street, Blinkton
7203 4614
Mrs. Bloggs
Provides volunteers/one trip per week
per person/old person must be really
desperate/needs letter confirming
In her office Tues. Wed. & Thurs. AM only

Figure 4.2

may need encouragement and they will often need support
through an appeal given the extent to which appeals seem to
be necessary. Older volunteers trained in welfare benefits
work are an invaluable source of help in this field because they
can relate to the unease about claiming and they can sometimes share their own experience usefully.

Housing is another complex area. Social workers should
know what is available from housing departments and housing associations. We should be able to give people correct
information rather than subjecting them to a trail of false clues
which lead nowhere. The housing association scene, for example, is particularly volatile and it is always worth asking
clients to report back so that you have an accurate picture.
Criteria for eligibility, the number of nominations accepted off
the corporation waiting list and the degree of frailty accepted
are the sorts of things which vary from scheme to scheme, and

which change frequently. Getting better accommodation for elderly people often seems a matter of being in the right place at the right time, but if this cannot be managed social workers can make sure that people are not sent off on a wild goose chase. Housing for old people can be normal tenancies, but it can also be in sheltered accommodation or amenity housing. Amenity flats or houses as they are described in Scotland are those easily accessible to older people because they are on the ground floor or have a lift. They also have whole house heating and safety features to meet the needs of older people. This concept is similar to Gategory 1 sheltered housing in England and Wales. Sheltered housing is basically the same physically although in older schemes there can be stairs up to the first floor. These flats or houses will be generally linked to a warden by an alarm call system and will have a laundry room and communal lounge areas.

Both councils and housing associations tend to be unwilling to be pinned down on their criteria for eligibility, but in my experience it is worth persuading elderly clients who want this sort of facility to put their names down on every possible list, while making sure that this does not raise their hopes unfairly. A single man is often easier to place than a woman because most housing schemes like to have a mixture and most applicants are women. For a fuller discussion of the issues surrounding sheltered accommodation, see Butler *et al.* (1983) and Middleton (1988).

To digress for a moment, sheltered accommodation has been seized on by caring professionals and relatives as the answer to all our problems. Old people claim they like it because they see it as an alternative to long-term residential care. Research studies like the two mentioned above indicate that it is suitable for only a proportion of the elderly population who like communal-type living and the institutional qualities that are inevitable when large groups of people are housed with a warden. The large numbers of people on waiting lists are usually escaping from housing problems rather than wanting specialist housing. Other resources ought to be adapted so that old people can be offered a proper choice of suitable accommodation. Imagination is required in terms of aids and adaptations to existing property, insulation grants, chemical toilets, new types of tenancies and so on. Box files should have a lug labelled ADAPTATIONS with a list of workshops for the handicapped and school woodwork departments who will install a banister or build a ramp. Chemical toilets can be provided and are accessible when someone is ill or when it is hazardous to go upstairs to a cold bathroom in the winter. A list of suppliers is needed. Shared tenancies or housing with a special care component do not suit many people, but for those for whom the alternative is residential care they provide an opportunity to live relatively independently. A list of associations that provide joint or special tenancies for elderly people should be on a card.

It is absolutely essential to be sensitive to the different life experience and expectations of different ethnic groups. The concept of a group home with a daily visiting housekeeper, for example, can work very with elderly Somali seamen. It can work a lot less well with, say, Chinese women who view anything except living with their families as a rejection and contrary to deeply held views of filial piety. The card system must have sections for all the different ethnic groups likely to request assistance and the specialist help available. (Some of these cards may be blank. Glendinning and Pearson (1988) in their digest of the literature about services for black and ethnic minority elders found evidence of extensive unmet need.)

These are only a few examples of the kinds of ideas that should be part of social work thinking on housing. One final tip: always ask if the housing is 'barrier free' which means that it will be suitable for people with disabilities. We have got to push housing providers into much more provision of barrier free housing so that the housing can suit the changing needs of older people.

With new sources of short-term finance for projects it is often hard to know what new services are available, and there is no answer to this beyond keeping an ear to the ground, and following up every possibility. It is better to be in at the start of a new service because early applications are always more likely to be successful. It always seems to take about a year for a service to get started, and waiting lists soon develop.

So we have our client, we have our index of services, and we now have to match the two. This is no easy task. Some people are clearly eligible for things that they will not accept, some demand everything possible, while others seem to need things that are not available. Let us take the first group. Persuading people to accept help is often a delicate task. For reasons already discussed, some people consider it a symptom of failure; others refuse because they do not fully understand what is available, and others refuse because they know only too well the second-rate quality of what is offered.

Coming to terms with greater dependence is one adjustment to failure that many old people have to make, and it can need a lot of talking through. Services like home helps or day centres may need to be very carefully offered. We should also be quite certain that we know what it is that we are providing. It is much easier to sell a service to an unwilling client if we *know* everything about it, or perhaps if we are there to make the necessary introductions. Mrs Roberts was recently widowed and very lonely indeed. She refused, however, to go to the very active and successful local day centre. She said she had never in her life attended a social gathering on her own. Social workers often underestimate the degree of fear elderly clients face when admission to hospital or a day centre is proposed. A consultant geriatrician I know says he has never known people refuse admission to hospital, but he always promises that he will be caring for them himself if they do come in. We could involve officers-in-charge of old people's homes and day centres much more actively to explain their establishment and to reassure elderly people, for whom admission to anywhere is a frightening step towards greater dependence.

A classic example of why some people might not understand what they are being offered is supplied by the case of Mrs Smith, who was given a stocking aid to help her pull up her tights because she was so arthritic she was unable to bend. The instructions were in German. A rail to help her up the stairs was delivered with two screws and no instructions. To help her sit up in bed she was also given a rope pulley, with the ropes hopelessly knotted together, so that it was impossible to see what it was. Old people often refuse even temporary stays in residential care because it feels to them like admission to the workhouse. They will not have been aware of the dramatic changes in residential care in the last fifty years or so. In her delightful book about group work with elderly people in hospital, Joan Cooper (1980) describes a group which discussed services, among other things. The old people were able to explain to each other what to expect from services and to seek an explanation from Miss Cooper when they were puzzled. In one session, for example, one old lady who had a home help explained to another that they were not busybodies but were warm and sympathetic helpers.

Timing and presentation of help are also crucial if services are to be accepted. As far as possible, services should be explained by one familiar and trusted person at a time when the old person is calm enough to listen and ask questions. Instead, we provide services through all kinds of different channels but with little coordination. Another sad and true story concerns Mrs Collins, who received six callers on the day she returned from hospital. She was much too queasy to deal with any of them, sent them away, and ended up waiting for weeks for services she badly needed.

Finally, a group not often mentioned: those who refuse the offer of services because they do not like them. Who can blame them? The most appalling degree of boredom exists in some day centres and day hospitals. Meals on wheels are often very stodgy and hopelessly dull. They may even sometimes be provided to clients who cannot eat what is given for religious and cultural reasons. This lack of sensitivity is inexcusable. Long-term residential and nursing home care can be a life sentence of insensitive institutional care, and social workers themselves are often hasty, offhand and unreliable.

People who demand everything possible elicit considerable antagonism from providers of social and health services. Yet they often only get what they are entitled to. We should ask ourselves why we get so exasperated, and also why clients are being so demanding. Sometimes the reason for this is easy enough to understand, though still difficult to deal with. Miss Fox, for example, had been the senior history teacher in a grammar school for girls. She was a tough, unlikeable woman who had devoted her whole life to her work. She was crippled by severe arthritis some ten years after she retired. Up to that point she had enjoyed her retirement, spending most of it as an active friend to her local museum and historical society. Confined to her flat, nobody came near her. The flat was grand and rather inconvenient. She was very demanding of her long-suffering neighbours and eventually of her home help and voluntary visitor. She complained about every effort made on her behalf, and nobody was ever brave enough to tackle her in a forthright fashion. This unpleasant woman was disliked throughout her social services office and health centre, without any of the countless people involved getting together and confronting the fact that although they felt desperately sorry for her, they all disliked her intensely.

Short-term funding can mean that some services are available only for a few years. Sometimes when the projects are part of employment initiatives the people employed change all the time. An important rule of thumb is that short-term funding is incompatible with long-term relationships. It takes time for communities to learn about and then to trust local projects. If they then disappear as funds run out then untold damage is done. Many services for black and ethnic elderly people have been set up using short-term funding. This is a highly unsatisfactory way to provide essential services for some of the most disadvantaged groups of elderly people.

Some people need services which nobody provides. There are sadly relatively few kinds of assistance where flexibility is built in. The best known project is in Kent, where social workers can spend up to two-thirds of the cost of a place in an old people's home to keep someone at home if they would otherwise have to be admitted. Sir Roy Griffiths in his report *Community Care: An Agenda for Action* (1988) maintains that as major providers of care local authorities have lost sight of individual needs. He proposes the total flexibility of packages of care assembled from private, voluntary and statutory provision. With skilled social work involvement in these packages, this is a very exciting prospect as long as the best, rather than the cheapest, package can be provided. Given the time, resources and training to give each individual and their family a network of intensive care, which is constantly under review, this would have a major impact on keeping frail old people properly looked after in their own homes. Sir Roy fails, however, to understand that health care must be woven into this process from the beginning: in deciding what needs to be provided, who provides it, to what extent and so on. There is a danger too that the task of putting together packages of care will be seen as a simple task and would focus entirely on practical help with little choice for the older person. We are going to have to insist that social work and health care are integral to any package of care for frail older people. It is interesting that Sir Roy does not see local authorities as major providers at a time when there are increasing numbers of highly flexible services being provided by local authorities. Most home helps have traditionally provided a very flexible service of sensitive care but often in their own time and unofficially. Now we are seeing increasing numbers of care assistant type of workers employed to provide every kind of personal service as well as new kinds of home help trained and encouraged to meet a wide variety of personal needs. It would be a great shame if these innovations were jeopardised by changes in the way care is delivered to keep frail older people in their own homes.

Many services can be used more flexibly and many more ideas for better services have yet to be tried out and evaluated. There is a section on how social workers might do more in this area in Chapter 5.

5

Behind-the-Scenes Work with the Old Old

Helping the helpers

The strain of working with very old people can be considerable, as can the provision of their day-to-day care. The
reasons for this are obvious. Whereas most very old people are
normal adults with whom one can have a perfectly normal
relationship, the very old people we are most likely to meet are
those who have particularly severe problems. They will tend
to be very dependent people with severe physical or mental
infirmities, or people with major problems of resources, personality or behaviour. Combined with the extent of their
problems is their complexity. Often old people that we come
into contact with will have physical ailments, perhaps some
psychiatric disorder and probably a lack of relatives as well.
This severity and complexity of problems is hard enough to
deal with, but the real strain is in the limited extent of our
ability to help. The only solution may seem to be an admission
to residential care, but this may not be desirable. Miss
Gwenda Jones of Chapter 4, for example, presented the social
worker with an interesting set of problems which proved very
daunting. She was a severely arthritic old lady of 87 who lived
in a house much too big for her requirements. As a consequence of her arthritis she was unable to get out to shop, visit
her church or to socialise with her friends. Her stiffness
increased and there were signs of malnutrition despite meals
on wheels. She had neither money nor energy to spend on her
house, which was consequently cold and gloomy. Prolonged

71

isolation seemed to have made her rather paranoid, though she had always scorned her neighbours as being of a lower class. Thus she was very much on her own, in increasingly poor health and at risk of hypothermia. She was also quite without relatives locally. A proud, determined woman, she would not even consider a home help, let alone residential care. The social worker was understandably dismayed: where do you start? In a sense any acceptable sort of help would break the downward spiral, so the social worker began with housing, which was the one problem Miss Jones was keen to solve. This was a long-term project and the social worker had to live with a slowly deteriorating set of circumstances in other respects: a great source of worry.

In Miss Jones' case, as in many others, one of the major sources of strain is the harassment from colleagues both within social work agencies and outside. Miss Jones' GP was forever on the telephone demanding that something be done. The neighbours felt guilty as well as irritated and they wanted something done. The social worker's senior was concerned that Miss Jones might be found dead on the floor and she felt that the social worker should push Miss Jones into accepting a home help. Coping with and helping colleagues under these kinds of pressures will form the bulk of this chapter, but first a brief word on the subject of death.

A further cause of stress is the inevitability of death. Many very old clients will die while we are working with them. Many of them are actually dying, and most of them will die within a few years. Sustaining an optimistic approach can be very difficult in these circumstances, though research has shown that most old people feel optimistic about the future, however limited a period that might be.

A facile observation is often made that to be a social worker with the very old you have either to be a saint or totally thick-skinned and insensitive. This is of course quite untrue, though both types exist. The issue here is that perfectly ordinary social workers enjoy working with very old people but that there may be a special need for us to look after ourselves so that we do not become utterly exhausted or battered into insensitivity. We are not very good on the whole at looking after our own needs for support and encouragement, though we are light years ahead of doctors and nurses, both of these groups maintaining the myth of professional objectivity.

Using professional skills to help each other ought to be much more common than it is, the lament of most social workers tending to be that they can cope with their clients but their colleagues drive them bananas. The answers are known, but the difficulty is making time and finding the energy to deal with them. Let us look at a few.

First, *supervision*: this important organisational and management process is one of the really important contributions social work could make to the caring professions generally. Although derived from psychotherapy and the requirement to know yourself before you can help others, supervision has been usefully adapted in many social work agencies. Usually it is a flexible tool for a senior social worker to provide support, time for reflection, accountability to management, tuition, etc., in proportions required by the recipient. I do not believe any social worker can sustain a reasonable quality of work without it, though some social workers are using husbands, friends and colleagues in a somewhat *ad hoc* fashion when the formal sessions are not forthcoming. Supervision makes time for and legitimises the business of discussing what we are actually doing. Given the kinds of decisions made and the potential degree of influence social workers have, it is critically important that we take this time. Perhaps I should specify what I mean by 'supervision' since I am constantly at a loss for words when seniors tell me they offer supervision 'when it is asked for' or that they are 'always available'. Supervision is, first, a regular period of time of at least an hour at least once a fortnight when the spotlight is on social workers' practice. It is the commitment to this process that is significant if sessions are to be planned and thoughtful. Ideally time should be spent on routine work as well as complicated and stressful work so that a quality of planning and thought is given to the whole work-load. There is something about putting what you are doing into words that organises the experiences, allows the feelings to emerge and makes planning a more realistic possibility. Why the sudden evangelical quality to the text, you may be asking? The answer is that as a social work teacher I could tell within days which students had been getting proper supervision. It shows in the way that they approach a problem; purposefully and with consideration.

So what can be done if a social worker cannot get proper supervision from a senior? For a start I do not think that supervision necessarily has to be provided by a senior. Clearly this enables it to serve a double function because a senior does need to know what the social workers in her team are up to. But some teams use rotating supervision, claiming that it enables members of the team to pool their knowledge. In this case each social worker takes it in turn to supervise the team members and shares her particular way of looking at things, or her particular skills, with others. To get this going, however, presupposes a team in the first place, and if this is not the case, what then? Look elsewhere. There are a lot of people in other agencies, in universities and polytechnics, and people who have got time off from work who have small children, who will provide this help. Supervising is a stimulating and challenging process for the supervisor and can give enormous satisfaction. Some social workers have given and received supervision across professional boundaries. This is true for many hospital based social workers who are responsible in line management terms to other social workers but who receive help to reflect on work, tuition and support from medical and paramedical colleagues. Many social workers supervise occupational therapists, home help organisers, volunteers and project leaders. Similarly some residential social workers and child-guidance staff are supervised regularly by psychiatrists.

Another way of coping with stress and maintaining optimism is to set up a group. These can be informal like case discussions or formal like closed task-centred groups or regular meetings. The important thing is that they legitimise the time taken to share experiences, to offload feelings, to reflect on practice. Having worked as an isolated social worker in general practice and as someone who gains a lot from group experience, I have had each of these and found them worthwhile. They often seem to have a limited life and last only as long as the members share the need and the commitment. I suspect that as social workers become generally more skilled in group work we will be able to run groups for ourselves more efficiently. At the moment a great many groups like these founder on private agendas and individual needs which are never resolved.

So where can a supportive group be found? The answer is usually that the social worker sets one up, with all the difficulties mentioned in Chapter 4. They can be set up within or outside the agency, and there are advantages and disadvantages to each. Groups with members from different agencies take longer to settle as people get to know each other and longer periods of explanation are needed about different settings. It is probably advisable to devote at least one session to intensive 'getting to know you' exercises. It is certainly quite essential to clear up aims right at the start: they may be different but they must be compatible. I had a most disappointing experience of one of these groups, where one rather powerful member clearly wanted a personal growth experience, while other members wanted to discuss their work. Groups within agencies can move into action much more quickly since people know each other and share an understanding of the agency. Nevertheless, they can have disadvantages because of the parochial nature of the discussion, and the fears members may have about divulging too many of their weaknesses to their colleagues. All these difficulties must be sorted out at the start by rules of confidentiality and shared objectives.

One of the main difficulties of support groups, wherever they are held, is the need for time to attend. It is relatively easy if you work in a team, because a good team will know the importance of sharing and will give time for members to get together; it might even be part of the normal team activities to have case discussions or group supervision. It is much more difficult to get time off to attend a support group outside the agency. Sometimes time can be agreed as a period of training, but more often these groups occur at lunchtime or after work.

In the last paragraph I referred to the 'team,' a concept which deserves closer examination since it is much used and misused in social work. It is used to describe any group of people who work together or even those who meet periodically and talk together. It is used to give an impression that some important business takes place and that there is a high quality of interaction going on. 'Team' is one of those words too easily corrupted by social work, like 'care'. These words start out by describing good and useful things and degenerate through careless use into meaning nothing. A more thoughtful use of the word 'team' would describe a quite specific way a group of people work together. A proper team means the constructive pooling of knowledge and skills which provides a vastly enhanced service for the client. Malcolm Payne (1982) has written a useful book about teamwork.

As a rule of thumb, I think that a team is successful when people feel able to express negative feelings, either about their work or about each other, and the team can tolerate and deal with these constructively. To get a group of people who work together to function in this way is very hard indeed. Interprofessional teams have been studied more thoroughly than some professional ones in studies like the one on primary health care teams by Gilmore *et al.* (1974). Both sorts of teams are rare. They are rare not just because they need a degree of effort and commitment from all participants, but because a prerequisite is a degree of staff stability. Teams cannot get going in any real sense if staff turnover is high. Experience tells us that newcomers force teams to readjust themselves, and that there is a very real gap to be filled if anyone leaves. Teams also take time to develop, though this can be lessened if members are prepared to put in some effort. Some of the best teams I know speeded up the process by going away for a day or a week together. This may seem impossible to arrange. Cover for emergencies has to be organised, and staff may have to give up some of their precious work time. Yet those who have experienced being away from the office with their colleagues will always tell you that it was worthwhile. It gives them the opportunity to appreciate the internal dynamics of the group, and to sort out some of the issues that never get proper attention at busy staff meetings. To make the best use of a day away from the office it is important to have an agenda agreed in advance and to have minutes taken. These sessions need to be purposeful. In my opinion all groups who work together should have at least one whole day a year to stand back and appraise the group's work and to make plans for the next year.

Most social workers, however, work separately, coming together for meetings but not working as a group. Sometimes sub-groups of two or three social workers form a mini-team to help one another but they make little impact on the practice of the whole group. If a group of social workers seems to have potential as a team, then it is important for the individual worker that she thinks tactically. It is foolhardy to press for a team approach on your own, since the outcome will then depend on the degree to which other people respect your own judgement. More usefully, the social worker should seek an ally, and then work together on the others, starting if possible on the person you perceive as having the most influence on the group. Do not be misled into thinking that this is the noisiest. It may often be the quietest and most independent person who is most respected. Sometimes a team in the true sense of the word may not be possible. Groups of people who work together can be happy to work more closely without committing themselves to a shared policy and philosophy. Thus case discussions or training sessions can be very useful and cohesive with colleagues, without ever being team meetings as such.

It may, however, be necessary for us to look outside our colleague group. Sometimes groups set up for social workers, can be found, but more often there exist groups of people who meet together to talk about topics of mutual interest – support and discussion of practice not being overtly part of the business. The British Association for Service to the Elderly (BASE) groups, and the British Association of Social Workers' Special Interest Groups on Ageing (BASW/SIGA) are two possibilities. These often become support groups for social workers and others who need an opportunity to talk about the stresses of working with very old people with a group of people who share the experience. A great deal of work with the very old is done by isolated social workers in special units or specialist workers in generic teams. Greater efforts could usefully be made to get together collectively – the need is always demonstrated by the enthusiastic participation in conferences and seminars. On these occasions small groups always elicit harrowing personal experiences and professional difficulties.

If there is the need for such a meeting of minds and a lack of resources and contacts to get one going, it is usually worth tackling the local Workers' Education Association or Extra-Mural Department, who are only too keen to hear of demand for courses. This may sound a bit platitudinous, but I am always surprised how seldom people ask for courses to be put on and yet rush to join when one is provided. It always seems rather a waste of further education resources if the authorities are not told what people want.

So far this section has been about social workers finding ways of sustaining their morale in a difficult and demanding job. But how can we help colleagues in other agencies, neighbours, friends and relatives who are often in much closer contact and suffer much more extreme daily stress? In Chapter 3 I looked briefly at some of the needs of relatives who are themselves in their late 60s and 70s. At the start of this chapter I said that for social workers the stress was caused by the nature, extent and complexity of some of the problems met in this field. Death is also continually present and can make social work demoralising. These problems are shared by all the other caring professions and they are yet more acute for those providing day-to-day care. I want here to consider some of the extra strains imposed by prolonged contact.

Perhaps it would be a help to start by explaining what I mean by this last point. Caring for a physically sick or mentally infirm very old person can be a very stressful occupation (and I make no apology for again repeating this). Social workers have worked out a support system for themselves which, when it works well, is invaluable. Other professionals, like residential staff, doctors and nurses, have not given enough attention, in my opinion, to the personal toll that prolonged stress take of them. There are signs of change, however, and there have been several attempts to deal with this – more often for people who work with children and families than for those who work with elderly people. The stress for relatives, neighbours and friends is often the greatest, and far too little is done to help them in their efforts. First of all we need to know what it is the carers need. And this question is seldom asked because there is so little that can be offered. Carers struggle on because they do not know who to ask and what to ask for.

Let us start with a relative. Mr Johnson was a bachelor in his 50s who had been caring for his mother in her 80s in a respectable suburban house which possessed every comfort. He worked in the local authority personnel department and was a respected and well-liked man with many friends. After his mother's death, Mr Johnson took up voluntary work with elderly people, and surprised himself and the other participants when he broke down and wept in one of the training sessions. He said he was weeping for the terrible couple of years before his mother's death, when she became very disorientated as well as very frail. She would wander about the house at night, crying out and stumbling into things. She went to a day centre during the day until she became bedfast, but this meant that Mr Johnson had to get up early to get her ready. His social life became more and more limited as he was forced to stay in at weekends and in the evenings to care for his mother. He said she had been a wonderful woman, and when she was quiet and calm he was able to love her. But when she was disturbing him in the night he felt utterly helpless and full of terrible rage. This was exacerbated by lack of sleep. He could be disturbed two or three times a night and he had to get up and see that she was safely back in bed. Towards the end Mr Johnson said he was nearly incoherent with exhaustion and desperation. And for months after her death he could not sleep right through the night.

Mr Johnson's story is familiar. It illustrates several things. First, Mr Johnson did not know, initially, what was wrong with his mother or what to expect. Neither did he recognise his need for help. He felt he had a duty to his mother and a responsibility to care for her. He was visited frequently by the GP, who could do little except provide a mild sedative and treatment for Mrs Johnson's physical ailments. At the end the GP provided a district nurse who helped Mr Johnson change the bed and clean up his mother. She also organised a visit from the social services who arranged day care. Equipment like a commode and the incontinence laundry service were mobilised by the district nurse. For all this help Mr Johnson was extremely grateful. But he was unaccustomed to making demands for himself and so many of his needs went unrecognised. What were these needs? He needed information about his mother's illness: diagnosis, prognosis and management. He needed some opportunity to sustain his own social life and social contacts, to sustain his own personality. He needed a holiday occasionally to restore his health. He needed someone to talk to about the rage he felt towards his mother – he never actually hit her, but in his fury he was sometimes rough with her and was then stricken with remorse. He felt at the time unable to admit to these negative feelings – and certainly not to friends and neighbours. He also needed to feel he was not alone in his struggle to provide a reasonable ending for his mother.

Mr Johnson's experience is different only in a degree from the neighbour who calls twice a day, every day, without fail. A neighbour who cannot go on holiday or even away for the day without making elaborate arrangements. I once visited an elderly housebound woman who had spent two weeks in an old people's home, and when I saw her she was still burning with resentment. She said it was her neighbour who had sent her. The neighbour called in several times a day for shopping, helping her in and out of bed and occasional other chores, and this neighbour had gone to stay with her daughter who had just had another baby. The old lady was indignant – she had hated the old people's home and felt a victim of her neighbour's whims. It is not easy to be mature and reasonable if you are either dependent or depended on to any great extent. Both sides may need help in their efforts to keep the relationship positive and fruitful.

Neither is Mr Johnson's experience different from the home help's when she comes in regularly to clean up. Sometimes these visits can be a rewarding experience. Sometimes home helps have to cope with arrogance and criticism, or with quite disgusting cleaning jobs, and with terrible worries about the vulnerability of their clients. District nurses, too, may be visiting people regularly who cause them the most intense concern. They may also visit people who they find utterly objectionable. GPs can have very worrying times and ambivalent relationships with their patients. Perhaps one of the hardest feelings that all carers have to deal with is fury: at the filth, the ingratitude and the unreasonable demands and responsibilities thrust upon them. Violence towards very dependent people is not uncommon although it is very seldom recognised. Sometimes of course the violence is the other way. People with dementia can be quite physically fit and can strike out. Complicated feelings of guilt and anger run high.

It is really not surprising that one way carers cope with this stress is to demand removal of the old person. At a stroke the burden of care and worry is shifted to a hospital, nursing home or residential establishment – but shifted only to someone else. Residential staff cope with all the problems of care not only of one person but of dozens. The degree of stress in these circumstances can be quite overwhelming. At its simplest there is the impossibility of ever getting the basic needs of residents met. Evans *et al.* (1981) have done some research on the time it takes to get a group of frail elderly people to the lavatory: it seems to be that either you do nothing else all day or you allow people to wet themselves. The demands of caring for large numbers of very old sick people are immense, and can lead to just the kind of frustration and exhaustion felt by Mr Johnson, especially since staff often have to give up their free time in times of staff shortage. The personal toll this kind of prolonged care of groups of very frail old people can take is quite enormous. The high degree of sick leave in some residential establishments for old people is not at all surprising.

So what can social workers do to help? It is all too easy to back away, especially given the impossibility of meeting all people's needs in time of financial cutbacks on public services. First let us assume that the information index, described in Chapter 4, is available. So all the available information is accurate and up-to-date. Second, let us assume that we can direct the carer to someone who can provide basic and comprehensible medical information. In terms of more personal help to helpers social workers should clearly start by relating the lessons we have learned for ourselves to the other people caring alongside.

What Mr Johnson, the weary care assistant, the exasperated home help and the puzzled neighbour need is an opportunity to put all their complicated and uncomfortable feelings into words. It is not easy to own up to feeling angry, rejecting and even violent towards frail and dependent old people. But it is a tremendous relief to have done so. It is the intensely ambiguous nature of the feelings that make them so painful and unacceptable for people who provide day-to-day care for old people. To hate someone you normally like or even love is very traumatic. And usually after the expression of anger comes the realisation that there are rewards and that perhaps one can cope more sensibly and seek help with particular problems.

How can social workers provide these vital opportunities for listening? We can do it ourselves, but this requires making time available when people need it. Relatives and neighbours may be happy to talk if social workers are clearly interested and sympathetic, and can be trusted not to rush to judgement. But social workers are obviously unable to meet the vast potential demands in the community and we ought to be helping other people to provide. The clergy, for example, are skilled at listening, and some of them are already involved in counselling. They are quite accustomed to dealing with emotionally charged situations. But perhaps more of them need alerting to this new needy group. Projects and agencies offering family casework or counselling may need to look more carefully at the three or four-generation families they will be meeting. Too often the attention is focused on the adolescent when it is the grandmother who is causing the strain. Somehow it is all right to be angry with a 15 year-old but not with a frail 90 year-old. And social workers will collude with this since most of us will have much more experience with teenagers. There is also some pressure from social work social services departments to focus on children in trouble in preference to their grandparents. Social workers must beware of being the arbitrators in irreconcilable conflicts of interest between carer and cared for. This relationship can be as emotionally loaded as any marriage. Conciliation is required in many situations but in some there seems no way through. We tend to side with the carer – with whom we can feel much more empathy. We ought to consider in these circumstances a properly negotiated outcome where each side concedes something and retains something.

Sometimes in negotiation quite unexpected and imaginative outcomes can be achieved because the points of conflict are clarified properly. Negotiation does require each side to be represented – though not necessarily by a social worker. This way of working is recognised in marital work and in conflicts of interest involving children when there are invariably two workers. It is time that conflicts of interest between carer and cared for were recognised as having the same sorts of tensions and the same importance for the individuals involved.

I am not sure what a social worker's role might be with professional colleagues like doctors, nurses and home helps who are feeling the strain, since social workers have no mandate to counsel and support exhausted colleagues. I know that it helps to be aware that they do not have the support systems built into their jobs as many of us have. Sometimes it enables us to cope with a doctor who goes temporarily off her head and shouts all her resentment at you, acknowledging only at the end of it that you may be equally helpless. It helps to understand and sympathise, but what can social workers actually do to help? Once again the answer may be to look carefully at some of the under-used capabilities of people in training sections, professional associations and HQ, though it may need a team effort to convince them that something has to be done. But once again the more viable alternative can be a group of some sort.

What does Mr Johnson get from a group of people in a similar position? He gets information, he escapes from his mother for a couple of hours, he gets some recognition of the important task he has set himself, and he is allowed to express his feelings and share them with people who feel just the same. He can even laugh, an experience carers often mention as important in their groups.

Self-help groups for carers are only slowly being recognised as one of the most under-used resources. Setting them up does take time and trouble, but it is well worth it. The main problem for Mr Johnson in joining such a group is finding someone to mind his mother for him. Some day centres run groups which is one way round this problem. Sometimes, if it is only for a couple of hours, relatives or friends can be persuaded to look after the aged relative. Granny-sitting schemes do not seem very successful because people are often unwilling to leave their relatives with strangers. If the family is linked to a volunteer scheme or a church, something can sometimes be done. Extra effort is needed but is immensely worthwhile. I visited a lady in her 50s who said that the group she had attended was the only thing that kept her sane while she was caring for her mother. I also set up and ran a five-session group for relatives of patients with dementia while working in a psychogeriatric hospital in Victoria. The relatives were very appreciative, indeed I received a grateful letter from a niece many months later. Interestingly what these relatives wanted more than anything was a full discussion of the diagnosis and prognosis. They were intensely relieved to find that the strange behaviours they had had to deal with were common symptoms of dementia and that the other people in the group had had the same experiences. Isolation and desperation was a common experience and I wondered if they might have cared at home for a longer period had they had the information and support they needed. These groups need to be offered much more widely and to be properly evaluated. There are plenty of descriptions of how they have been run successfully in social work journals but there is no authoritative review available.

Groups for colleagues and fellow professionals are difficult to set up. In Liverpool I helped to run a monthly group for people working with old people, and a wide range of professions and some volunteers joined. Courses, too, can provide an opportunity for mutual sharing and support. I have taught on extra-mural courses ostensibly set up to teach something quite specific, but I found that the students were keen to share their anxieties about their work. More and more of these courses should be run. One-day courses, short courses and regular evening classes all attract different people and meet a clearly demonstrated need. Sometimes courses are best run for people with the same job, like wardens of sheltered housing, and sometimes they are best mixed. The advantage of the former is the shared understanding of the agencies and the likely problems. The disadvantage is the parochial quality that creeps in and the way stereotyped approaches can be reinforced. Mixed groups can inspire a recognition that problems are shared and that the solutions may need some quite fresh, joint way of looking at the problem. Training sections in social work agencies do far too little on the whole to provide opportunities for sharing worries and gathering new ideas, and if they start at all they are often for fieldworkers rather than residential staff or home helps.

Training in itself can be an immense help to helpers who may have been causing themselves a lot of extra effort through sheer lack of knowledge. This can be in the physical sense of not knowing how to lift old people in a way that minimises the strain on back muscles. It can be in the emotional sense in that they do not understand, say, the way that some medication affects old people's behaviour. Training, too, can change attitudes. A good example of this is given by Veronica Coulshed (1980), who as a hospital social worker instituted training sessions for nurses in reality orientation techniques. The effect was to raise the level of interest and care given by the nurses and to increase morale vastly. All of us can use constant training to keep us alert and positive, but some groups seem to do particularly badly as far as training is concerned, and it may be that we can share what we know with groups like home helps, day-centre staff and volunteers. In geriatrics those who have least seem to get least, and this applies to training opportunities as well. This is an area where social workers could make a real contribution if we saw training as one of our responsibilities. It need not be anything high-powered – regular case discussions can be enormously helpful.

Finally, I want to look at practical services. Much of what was mentioned above (pp. 60) applies here, but we should perhaps give extra attention to the notion of *respite*. Most people carry on if they have something to look forward to – and this is usually some break in the burden of caring. Holidays are a comfort and are looked forward to, as well as being needed, by social workers. Many carers cannot have holidays, because they cannot afford them (and it costs more if money has to be found for grandmother to go somewhere). Often a hospital is the only possibility and some geriatric and psychogeriatric units have a few beds used exclusively for short-term relief for carers. Many old people's homes offer this

service but often in a rather casual fashion. Arrangements are
made at the last minute and there is no opportunity for the
relative to visit the home and be reassured that the care is
adequate. A holiday can be completely spoiled if it is spent
worrying about an elderly mother and whether the home will
be able to cope. Social workers are often responsible for
arranging these short-stay admissions and do not always give
them the care they deserve. It can make all the difference to
the success of the stay if the elderly person goes into a place
that is familiar and welcoming. An unsuccessful short-term
admission to a hospital or residential establishment can mean
months of readjustment afterwards and a real fear of being left
again. Boarding out can be an alternative for people like Mrs
Dickens, who was 87 and lived with her daughter Mrs Foot
and her husband and four children. She was crippled with
arthritis and needed a great deal of personal care. Usually
Mrs Dickens went for two weeks to a convalescent home
which she knew and liked. This closed down due to lack of fire
precautions, and she was able to go for a couple of years to a
home run by the local authority. They could no longer take
her. Mrs Foot was quite frantic. The GP was unwilling to
provide a hospital bed; indeed, he doubted that this would be
possible. Finally, Mrs Dickens was referred to a voluntary
agency running a short-term boarding-out scheme for elderly
people. She now goes twice a year to the same family. The
family's house is convenient for Mrs Dickens, and they are
well able to cope with her needs for personal care. Arrangements are made well in advance, which gives both families
time to plan the stays. When I spoke to Mrs Dickens she was
delighted with the arrangement. Interestingly when I suggested to her that she might have preferred someone moving
in with her to look after her, she agreed wholeheartedly. This
is very rare except between friends and relatives. Most people
assume it is impossible because of the obvious difficulties of
leaving a stranger in your home while you are away. But it is
not impossible as the Liverpool Personal Service Society have
shown with their boarding-in scheme. They provide increasing numbers of carers willing to go and stay with a frail elderly
person. This is especially beneficial to people who are blind or
confused for whom moving elsewhere can be a major up-

heaval. The relocation research shows us that a move, especially one that does not make sense to someone who is very frail, can be detrimental to physical and mental health. The Liverpool Personal Service Society believe the secrets of their success are no different from the secrets of the success of their boarding-out scheme: very careful matching and lots of round-the-clock support. They also stress that carers do not all function at the same level. Skills can be built on but one of the matching factors is matching carers to what they can deal with.

So, in summary, carers are the most valuable resource we have for looking after sick, very old people. Three ways of helping them seem particularly valuable: opportunities to talk and share their worries, opportunities to obtain good information and opportunities to get away for a while, whether for two hours or two weeks.

Dealing with ageism

As I said at the start, ageism is rife in society. Social workers are both culprits and victims. We are culprits because we often collude with the second-rate service given to old people, and victims because as social workers with a special interest in old people our career opportunities are often diminished. The first task must be to raise all social workers' consciousness of yet another 'ism' to be aware of. This is difficult because ageism is so fundamental in society. However, without this consciousness social workers will not be ready to change attitudes. Unless attitudes change, we will never substantially improve the position of old people in society.

I am resisting the temptation to speculate on why we all dread growing older. It is too easy to speed into a diatribe on the penalties of materialism or the obsession with economic growth, and to ignore the paradox that it is because of industrialisation, the Empire and other unsavoury characteristics of our history and society that we have such a large older population. And this same history means that we too will live into our 70s and 80s. So while not wishing to belittle the search for the causes of ageism, I want to concentrate on what it is.

Ageism, like racism and sexism, is about prejudice against a section of the population. And prejudice is about ignorance, deprivation of power, stereotyping, and so on. Ageism, like the others, is internalised by the victims who can share the stereotypes. But ageism is curiously unlike the others in that we cannot experience another's race or sex, but we shall all (or most of us) experience old age. Another curious paradox emerges: we shall all experience old age and yet we all pretend that this is not the case. The cover-up is subtle. We nurse a stereotype of passivity in old age, of less demands for food, for sex, for power, for status. The stereotype has a belittling effect – 'little old lady', 'old biddy', 'elderly gent', and so on. The stereotype suggests less competence, both physically and intellectually. The existence of people who conspicuously contradict the stereotype does nothing to minimise it. If they are seen as extraordinary exceptions, then the stereotype of normal old age continues. This is no different from the way that the single powerful black person or the individual influential woman does nothing to alleviate prejudice to these groups. While going along with the stereotype of old age, most people do not see themselves ever being a 'little old lady' or an 'old codger'.

The process of acquiring these negative attitudes starts as soon as we are adults. How often have you said or felt that the reason you were puffed going up the stairs, or the reason that you keep forgetting things is because of increasing age. (Admittedly this explanation is also a useful excuse because there is nothing you can do about advancing years, whereas you could keep more fit or try harder to remember things.) But all the time in our daily conversations we are underlining for ourselves and for other people that as you get older you get less competent. And this is quite untrue. Research (Naylor and Hardwood, 1975) has shown that 70 year-olds can be taught German as quickly as 15 year-olds, albeit by different teaching methods; and 60 year-olds have taken up long-distance running. Vast numbers of elderly people feel optimistic and enthusiastic about their future, and yet younger people face the prospect with dread. And it is this dread, I think, that makes people avoid any serious discussion about growing older. Negative feelings are revealed in odd insulting remarks about people being too old for their jobs, and so on. But these are seldom questioned or the serious evidence about competence in old age examined.

Social workers must be in the business of consciousness raising because they are in such a strong position to see the consequences of ageism. At the simplest level, consciousness raising is about protesting every time someone makes an ageist remark. The next time someone says the reason they cannot remember telephone numbers like they used to is because they are getting older, suggest that she did not have as many other things to remember when she was younger! Or when someone complains that their joints ache and it must be the onset of age, suggest that perhaps it is a result of being overweight or not getting enough exercise. More commonly, however, among our colleagues ageism is very subtle. A senior social worker spoke at some length to a meeting, when describing the advantages of specialisation, about the fact that old people do not need social workers. He told us, without any shadow of doubt, that what they need is kind caring people like volunteers and home helps. When questioned it transpired that he had always worked with children and families. He had no experience of the way old people benefit from good social work help. He had no knowledge of the kinds of interpersonal and complex practical problems that old people have. He was ready to admit that some of the families he worked with did not appreciate or show any noticeable improvement from intensive social work. But the thought that they might need a kind volunteer or a home help was unacceptable. We also thought that he was underrating the quality of care given by home helps, but this is not the place to develop that theme.

Sometimes, sadly, it seems as if people like this senior social worker actually dislike old people or are in a curious way frightened of them. When I ask groups of social workers what they dislike about old people I am sometimes struck by the vehemence of their replies, like 'I hate wrinkled and scaly skin', and 'I hate their smell'. Obviously some people have had very bad personal experiences of elderly people: perhaps their grandparents. It is a good idea to get them to tell you about this aversion at the outset. Cherry Rowlings (1981) has an excellent section on this in her *Social Work with Elderly People*.

Thus at a personal level we must be alert: it is quite surprising how once consciousness is aroused ageism can be found everywhere. But the issue is more than a personal one. Every day policy decisions are being made to limit the quality and quantity of resources for elderly people. Whereas this is true generally (see the recent history of the old-age pension), I want to stick to social welfare resources. The best way to see such discrimination is to compare resources for elderly people with those available for children. While I do not want to argue that children should not be a priority, the extent of the difference in quality and quantity of resources is quite inexcusable. Look first at the qualifications and experience of social workers with the two groups, then at the amount of training time, then at the range of alternatives to home care, and then at the actual quality of residential care – staff pay, qualifications and status, assessment, admission and review systems. The evidence is unequivocal – old people are not seen to need or deserve a fair share of the social services cake.

Yet some people will say that services for old people eat up the bulk of social services expenditure. So they should. But the amount of money spent on one child in care is much greater than that spent on one old person in care. The difference in overall proportions of the budget is a reflection of the different numbers of needy individuals. Others will say that we have no legislation for old people that makes specific requirements as it does for children. This, too, must be a consequence of ageism, but it is also that the law that does exist is interpreted much more generously for children.

And so it goes on. I have rehearsed here only one or two arguments because of limited space, and because I want to illustrate that social workers who are interested in old people must go on the attack. Ageism is so subtle that it is easy to go along with decisions without realising how many of them are based on ageist assumptions about the worth of elderly people. Social work with old people should not be a refuge for shrinking violets: it ought to attract the most assertive and vociferous social workers, because there is a cause to be fought for.

And what about old people themselves who have internalised many of the negative stereotypes? This is far more difficult and complicated to tackle, for several reasons. First, it is because people who are old today have survived some very troubled times. The deprivations of the Great Depression, for example, make the receipt of a regular, if ungenerous, income a relative luxury. Second, most very old people are women and they have always seen their role as 'making shift' and adjusting themselves to the vagaries of history and their menfolk. For them, too, the regular pension is more money to spend on themselves than many of them have ever had. They are not accustomed to making demands of anybody, and they consider it a matter of intense pride not to ask for more of anything. Thrift is one of the skills of which they are most proud. Third, older people, unless they have been in trade unions, are not used to organising themselves to demand more for pensioners. They can of course be organised given support initially as the successful work setting up Strathclyde Elderly Forums has shown (see Melling *et al.* June–July 1986). Many of them believe that old people are less important and of less worth than wage earners and their families. Their full power as voters at the very least has yet to be recognised: 25 per cent of the electorate in some inner-city areas are retired, and the figure is as high as 30 per cent in some seaside towns. However, Midwinter and Tester's report on the 1987 election shows that elderly people tend to vote on issues of national concern such as health and defence rather than on the basis of self-interest.

I am not sure what will raise the consciousness of our elderly population, whether social workers should be setting up older versions of women's groups, or whether the media could play a bigger role. This in fact may be happening. There has been a small increase in the numbers of television plays in which old people are shown as leading absorbing lives of intrigue, romance and excitement, rather than being passive, dependent and boring. But I do feel that social workers who know a lot about older people's circumstances should accept the responsibility to do what they can to provide information and ideas to elderly people themselves, and to avoid reinforcing low expectations and feelings of worthlessness. It is of course much easier to condone low expectations when rationing inadequate resources, but social work is not for people who want an easy life. The least we can do is apologise constantly for what little is offered, and to make sure that people understand what is going on. Cuts have hit older people in receipt of social services much more than they have hit services for children at risk. They have hit doubly hard because the numbers of elderly people have been going up as the services have diminished. Even in areas where services have held their own or improved slightly, they have never increased in the same proportions as the population of very old people.

In summary, then, social work must involve changing attitudes, and in our own limited way social workers must tackle ageism wherever it is found. This is a skilled business involving knowledge, experience and an ability to explain how things really work. But before ageism can be tackled we must raise our own consciousness and those of colleagues and old people.

Generating and organising resources

Our role in generating and organising resources is going through a period of radical change at the moment. With the expansion of the private sector and increasingly significant involvement of the voluntary sector, social workers have had to improve their skills in relating to this effectively. Sir Roy Griffiths' report *Community Care: Agenda for Action* (1988) already mentioned in Chapter 4 takes this a step further. He does not want social service authorities, as he calls them, being primarily providers of services. He wants them instead to assess needs, set priorities and objectives and develop local plans. He sees our job as arranging packages of care dovetailing help from numerous authorities. He does see our role as designers, organisers and purchasers of non-health care services. He emphasises consumer choice, innovation and efficiency. Whatever happens to this report we will always be in the business of designing and organising services.

At present social workers continually organise resources behind the scenes even if we do not generate them, and yet

very seldom do these efforts receive enough planning and
evaluation. This may be because we are not entirely sure
whether this is our job or whether it ought to be 'management's'. It may also be because it requires one to stand back
from the daily grind to see what is needed, what resources are
available and how these might best be mobilised. Outcomes
are often very distant. It can, for example, take a couple of
years to get a house converted as a shared tenancy for confused elderly people. Yet this can be a very rewarding kind of
social work, and can help basic-grade social workers feel that
they are doing more than keeping a finger in a rapidly disintegrating dyke.

I do not want to spend time here suggesting how resources
might be best allocated, but instead I want to concentrate on
how to generate services to meet the gaps. Resources have
always had to adapt to some extent because of changing
demands since the postwar 'Welfare State' legislation. The
home help service is a classic example of this. Originally set
up to help mothers newly returned from hospital with their
babies, it has become a flexible and sensitive service maintaining old people in their own homes.

Social workers in day-to-day contact with elderly people
ought to be in the vanguard of efforts to adapt and improve
resources. We should not be content with simply assessing
eligibility for existing resources. We should first of all be
trying to get an accurate picture of what people need. As
people who supposedly have particular skills in listening and
starting from the clients' perception of need, social workers
should be hearing what they are saying. This must of course
be balanced against what relatives, neighbours and fellow
professionals are saying. Often it is the employers' needs that
are paramount; hence saving money or the difficulties of
obtaining new money seems to be a preoccupation that instantly petrifies any initiative. It need not have this effect.
Some of the most imaginative schemes have arisen because
they are cheaper than alternatives, particularly when they are
alternatives to residential care. I do not intend to say that
social workers should find *exactly* the right service for every
single client. Social work has always been about compromise.
It does sometimes look, however, as if clients have to do most

of the compromising. They have to adapt to inflexible criteria for eligibility or rigid rules in residential establishments and day centres, as well as to constant diminution of services.

In terms of skills I do not think there is much to choose between those needed for adapting an existing resource and those for setting up a new one. The skills that are required are best described as 'entrepreneurial' in both instances. They concern lateral thinking, putting people together, helping them consider new ways of doing things, selling new ideas and sustaining an optimism that things can and will get better. First, I want to look at a couple of examples before going on to give some advice on how this entrepreneurial style of social work is most successfully practised.

I want to start with an example of an adaptation of a resource: long-term residential care. Strathclyde Regional Council Social Work Department found themselves with an old people's home with a day centre room incorporated into the building which was too small to use for day care on any scale. Dementia had been identified as an issue in both the home and the community, so it was decided that the small scale was right for day care for people with dementia. Simultaneously some extra money became available. The political argument had previously been made and won. This was a small amount of new development money to meet needs of people with dementia and their carers. This day centre was made one of the projects: the money being spent on a small staff team of three full-time staff, equipment and the much appreciated minibus.

The staff of the day centre are on the staff of the home and the organiser is supervised by the officer-in-charge. The centre takes eight people per day all of whom have to have a written diagnosis of dementia and have to be approved by a local multi-disciplinary team following a full assessment by a social worker. The centre took time to develop with a lot of inappropriate referrals initially. After considerable outreach work it is now thriving, able to provide day care between 8 a.m. and 8 p.m. by working shifts. Carers are intensely involved as is the home help service which will not only get people ready for the bus but will be at home to welcome the person with dementia again if this is required. The day centre staff do all the driving of the minibus and thereby are able to liaise directly with home helps and relatives. The bus is also used for outings all the time and is a vital tool for winding people down if emotions are running high. It is also built into the day's programme, for example to stimulate reminiscence by visits to old haunts. People with dementia have days to suit their needs and the needs of their carers. Two days are reserved for people with less severe dementia. Now the centre is running, attenders are being reviewed every six weeks. People's needs are changing constantly so this is essential, so too is an occasional overnight bed if an attender is for some reason distressed or carers cannot cope. The skills of the three staff are developing very rapidly. They are committed to the concept of a regular timetable which takes account of the tempo of the day. Their skills can then be shared within the home where there are several long-term residents with dementia and with the carers. This kind of small-scale flexibility is hard won and has involved a lot of work with the staff of the home and the centre. However, an invaluable resource has been created, which unlike many pioneering initiatives, has good support for the staff built in from the start.

A vital prerequisite for the success of this venture is the commitment of staff including top management and the local area office. Others are patience and determination. This project started up when a lot of reorganisation and staff changes were going on. It survived with gritty determination from key individuals who were sure that it could succeed. Skills of assessing and working with people with dementia have had to be acquired very rapidly and refined with practice. This centre could have been a storeroom, instead with vision, some cash and a lot of hard work it is a unique resource. There is, of course, an excitement about new projects in the field of dementia because so many pioneering initiatives are taking place. Thankfully, this particular project is being evaluated by a researcher based in a local training college so the lessons learned will be more widely available in due course.

I want now to look at a new resource to see what lessons can be learned, in this case from a housing association with a strong commitment to innovatory forms of community care. This housing association had set up a neighbour support scheme for very severely handicapped adults some three years previously when it obtained support finance (the Scottish version of joint finance) to employ two project workers to develop another scheme for severely disabled people and to extend the model to mentally handicapped adults and frail elderly people. This followed several meetings of housing, social work, medical and nursing activists evaluating the original scheme and discussing its applicability to other groups. Neighbour support operated in this association on the basis of three to six people (depending on whether people wanted to share flats) needing support and four neighbours providing support on a rota basis. The supporting neighbours are paid by the supported neighbours at roughly the same hourly rate as a home help from attendance allowances, grants and services charges. They provide a highly flexible service depending on the needs of the person needing care. They supplement the services already provided by home helps, district nurses, etc., and are on call 24 hours should emergencies arise. The planning group for the scheme for frail elderly people met fortnightly for 18 months working out criteria for eligibility, publicising the scheme, choosing supported neighbours and thinking through design features, ongoing support group systems and equipment needed for people with hearing, sight or voice problems. After supported tenants were selected they were consulted over any special adaptations or alterations needed to make the flats suitable to their needs. They were also involved with planning group members in drawing up criteria for, and interviewing and selecting their supporting neighbours.

We approached the whole venture with great caution always aware that the concept might not work with frail older people. We recognised that they are a group whose health and morale can change very rapidly, whose anxiety about participating in an experience can be high given their experience of moves in and out of hospital and for whom death is a real possibility.

All our fears were borne out. Our potential candidates were hard to find and several dropped out. One enthusiastic lady died suddenly, another was found to have cancer and is now living in a nursing home. But for the consistent enthusiasm of one very frail but very determined old lady we might have given up or changed the criteria. Mercifully we did neither and have now housed three very frail elderly people whose caring networks were disintegrating and for whom permanent institutional care was the next step. The flats are fitted with special equipment, including lavatories, to facilitate independence, and intercoms and alarm systems link to the supporting neighbours. The planning group has now finished its work and it will be up to the tenants to choose what sort of continuing support group they would like. Some informal support may be available from the other tenants in the block of flats in which this project is situated or from the sheltered housing scheme along the road. Sir Roy Griffiths (1988) exhorts us to limit the role of housing to the provision of bricks and mortar but often the provider of housing is well placed to weave care in with the bricks. Clearly in all these schemes substantial domiciliary care is provided by the health board and social work department, and attendance allowance by the DSS. But for both the supporting and supported neighbours provision of a secure, warm, good quality flat is an essential part of their participation in the project.

What are the lessons to be learned from this venture? First, that it is worth meeting and talking over a plan even if there seems little chance at the time of implementing it. The Association was ready with an idea as soon as they heard about the possibility of money becoming available. Second, you need to have some contacts with people who have some ideas about the availability of money. In this case the Association had very good links with both the health board and the social work department, though this is clearly not essential. In my experience news of available money goes round the voluntary sector like wildfire. Third, you have to be ready to strike while the iron is hot. This proposal was written and presented with great speed. Fourth, professional credibility is necessary: in this case a housing association with a good reputation was involved, and an application from them stood a good chance of being well regarded. Finally a great deal of time was put in to thinking through potential difficulties which means you are ready for setbacks. An extra bonus in this case was the willingness of a member of the university to monitor the scheme, which gave it extra status.

It might be assumed that these projects are much more easily set up within a voluntary agency, but this is not the case. Projects are springing up all over Britain, partly as a consequence of the pressure from diminishing resources within the social services, and partly because existing resources clearly do not meet the needs of elderly people. Schemes providing alternatives to residential care, like care assistants at home, putting-to-bed schemes, day care in old people's homes, visiting schemes, self-care networks, etc., abound. And most of these projects will have started with a small group of energetic people who were sensitive to the needs of their clients, were active in various other spheres which gave them access to news about money or changes in resources, and who were not complacent about current provision. Sadly these schemes are too seldom evaluated, so there is little real evidence as to which are the most successful projects. This means that mistakes are made time and time again (for an exception, see the work done at Kent University by Challis and Davies, 1980).

At this stage it might well be useful to provide a list of tips for social workers with an inclination to initiate change. First, never do it alone. Patti and Resnick (1975) make a special point of this. They suggest that social workers are more inclined to be reactive rather than proactive, but that it is foolish to be proactive individually, as you are likely to be too easily disregarded. The article by Patti and Resnick is valuable for anyone trying to produce change, and provides a clear possible strategy that should be very helpful for social workers keen to improve the service offered to clients.

Second, think beyond the agency. In most towns there seems to be a network of people who are energetic and committed to improving the care of old people. Perhaps they can be found in the local BASE or BASW groups. They will certainly be found at conferences and seminars. It only takes a small group of the right people. A local plan to provide a house for a shared tenancy for institutionalised elderly women, for example, had a tiny working party consisting of representatives of the institution's management and staff, and a housing association.

Third, prepare for a lot of talking before anything happens.

Papers are written and circulated, meetings held, and endless working and reworking of the ideas seem essential. An important principle here is that if there is opposition from particular people they have to be co-opted if at all possible. Sometimes this means showing them how the project will meet their needs, for example in terms of career advancement or national reputation. Seminars, films, visits to other areas where similar projects are successful are other ways of doing this, and can be valuable for all concerned. A group considering a self-care unit in an old people's home, for example, held several seminars for the staff, using film material at the local university, in order to be sure that all the staff fully understood what was being suggested and were able to voice their objections before any action was taken. Similarly, it can be helpful to invite someone from another area who has run a similar scheme to give a talk. To meet people who have actually achieved what is being attempted can be very reassuring as well as inspiring. It can also prevent some elementary mistakes.

Fourth, make use of other agencies as well as individuals. Could your project be an action research project? If this is difficult, could it at least be made more attractive by building in some formal monitoring by a reputable academic body? Are there other agencies who have needs that might be met along with yours? Projects, for example, that use unemployed young people or young offenders have a greater chance of success because they solve someone else's problems. Similarly, housing associations have been under some pressure to provide special projects, and a proposal to them would solve both sets of problems.

Finally, prepare for disappointment. Many projects never get off the ground, sometimes for quite predictable reasons, like opposition from key figures in senior management, or lack of money, and sometimes for no apparent reason. It is difficult to predict which projects will prosper; in my experience it is often the most unlikely that do. The moral is that you should not put all your eggs in one basket. I have always found that it is worth having more than one project on the go, since it sustains me when one falls by the wayside or is subjected to lengthy delays.

I shall conclude this section with examples of ventures

which make use of resources within groups of old people themselves. In the first a health visitor rather that a social worker plays the key role, but it could have been either. This health visitor got together with a very energetic caretaker in a cluster of high-rise blocks. These blocks were part of a dreary 1950s estate on the outskirts of a large town, and due to a city council policy not to put families in high-rise flats they were mostly full of old people rehoused after slum clearance. The old people were isolated and alienated. Our two activists recruited some tenants of the blocks, including some old people. A ground-floor section of unused pramsheds had been knocked into a single room for builders, and were swiftly colonised as a day centre. After a long and determined effort with some very colourful exchanges with various local authority departments, this centre is now a thriving focal point for the tenants of the flats. There are constant activities including bingo, meals, a chiropody session, bulk food buying, a health visiting session and hairdressing. The original group that got the day centre working is no longer central to the activities. These are run entirely by the residents and there have been many changes in key positions without the project faltering. Many old people have discovered new skills, new friends, a source of support in emergencies and a new sense of security.

Welfare benefits advice is essential to older people in deprived communities yet there are many barriers to be overcome. Older people are known to be anxious about claiming benefits for reasons of pride, fear of forms, lack of understanding of entitlement and so on. They are also often unwilling to seek advice from conventional advice centres which they see as part of the bureaucracy or intimidating in some way. Workers in the Age Concern Govan Project ran a very successful take-up campaign using older volunteers to break the ice and encourage their peers to seek advice. Subsequently this same group of older people set themselves up as Govan Action for Pensioners: a specialist advice service for older people. The Age Concern Govan project was able to provide an enormous amount of support and encouragement. They have also been very active in helping to organise training for the elderly people. Sometimes they have had to work alongside the elderly people to cope with the sheer volume of work arising from the changes in welfare benefits. Increasingly Govan Action for Pensioners is an independent group of highly skilled, well-organised and articulate older people. They have extended their service to a small pensioners flat and provide a much valued and very acceptable local re- source. The project has shown how intensive work at the start, building up skills and confidence, can be lessened over time. This sort of community work ought to be possible by any locally based community workers. Sadly, they often fail to see the resources among elderly people themselves and fail to understand how much more acceptable help is if it is given to older people by older people themselves.

In summary, this section on generating resources has fo- cused on change, either by adapting resources or by creating new ones. The aim has been to stress that this is possible and worthwhile. However, it takes a lot of skilful planning and preparation. This is true of any activity which involves groups of people, as we have seen, for example, in the description of group activities in residential settings. 'Entrepreneurial' seems the best word to describe the skills that are needed.

Working with other professionals

Working with other professionals is one of the inevitable delights of social work with old people. It can also be one of the most frustrating aspects of the work. It would seem sensible to start positively, but let me first explain the word 'inevitable'. Whereas younger people usually present us with one problem – a debt for example – old people's problems tend to be much more difficult to separate out. Their debt may be a consequence of an inability to get to the post office, which is a consequence of stiff knees, which are a consequence of a poor chiropody service, and so on. Perhaps this is because all systems function less well for elderly people. The notion of interlocking systems is certainly helpful: those within the old person in the bodily sense, those around the old person in terms of family, neighbours, housing, etc., and wider systems of the National Health Service, social services, etc. It seems with older people as if these are much more difficult to separate. There is of course the opposite way of looking at it: the way social workers classify people's problems and organise their services bears little resemblance to the kind of problems people have. By separating out older people's problems their fundamental wholeness and integrity are denied.

However, the fact remains that social workers cannot isolate themselves from other professionals in working with old people. For an old person at home the GP and the district nurse are always as important or more important than the social worker, and it is only by joint effort that a satisfactory service can be provided. An old person in hospital, if she is lucky enough to be in a geriatric unit, will benefit enormously from a joint case conference. Case conferences are a distinguishing feature of geriatric units and account in part for the success of this field of medicine. For the social worker this inter-professional work can be rewarding and stimulating. Equally, it can be hell.

What are the frustrations of working closely with other professionals? The first is that they see things differently, are employed by different kinds of agencies and have other priorities. Issues of status can also be major blocks to efficient co-operation. The ferment of hidden agendas and private struggles that bubbles beneath the surface of inter-disciplinary meetings can impede any satisfactory joint endeavour. Ignorance, jealousy and arrogance are only a few of the characteristics of some efforts at joint work.

Inter-professional teams working as such are very rare. Gilmore *et al.* (1974) looked at many primary care teams and concluded that very few were worthy of the name. Anthea Hey (1979) distinguishes between *teams* and *networks*, which is helpful since it is clearly possible to work with people in a positive but more distant way than in teams. For most social workers dealing with elderly people the experience of working with other professionals will be via neither teams nor networks, but on a one-off basis for particular old people. This can still be rewarding or frustrating and the skills required are to some extent the same.

What skills are required for successful working with non-social work colleagues? The main prerequisite has got to be commitment to making it work – playing to win and not playing at some private struggle. I really do think that some people relish the 'aggro' in multi-professional work. They work out long-standing resentments towards doctors, nurses or occupational therapists. They enjoy the baiting and excitement of the battles, and there is often a hidden sexual agenda since the doctors are so often men and the rest usually women.

Having decided to resolve rather than perpetuate the problems of inter-disciplinary work, the first skill is in tolerating the overlap. In any group of professionals there will be a high degree of overlap in the service offered to the client/patient. Elaine Murphy's (1986) description of the work of a psycho-geriatrician demonstrates a fine example of the overlap with social work. All the caring professions ought to be good at relating to people in distress, at organising services, and so on. You have to be able to tolerate what sometimes feels like removal of your particular role. At the same time, the individual has to know what she is particularly good at and be able to hold her corner. In some groups of professionals the social worker will have more skills in counselling than other participants, but this may not be the case, particularly if, for example, the GP is a disciple of Balint (1957) or the health visitor is a marriage guidance counsellor in her spare time. In my experience the social worker is often the one who can best grasp the whole person in context. Social workers know about the wider systems in which the old person lives – the housing, the finances, the neighbourhood. In these circumstances we have a special contribution to make in recognising and conveying the uniqueness and complexity of the situation.

A second essential skill for social workers working alongside other professionals is to understand how the latter view the situation. Social workers are supposedly able to do this for our clients but we seldom transpose these skills to relating to other professionals. How does a district nurse see an old person? Often it will be as a nursing problem – an ulcer to dress or an injection to be given. She will be aware of things that social workers might not even think about, like the pain the person may be feeling, or the way the ulcer may affect sleeping and walking. She will be conscious that timing is critical: dressings and injections have to be given when necessary, not when convenient. She will be aware of hygiene and the risks of infection, and of general health and healing capacity. She may also have enormous experience of nursing sick old people at home and be able to teach families how to do it, and to offer them comfort and reassurance. But from the social work point of view she may have quite different ways of looking at problems, and this must be appreciated. Part of this different way of looking at things can relate to the different ways professionals are employed. A health visitor, for example, will be employed in a hierarchical structure with a primary commitment to young children. A GP is to a large extent self-employed within constraints set by the NHS. She has no hierarchy but neither has she very much organisational defence if things go wrong, except via the Medical Defence Union. There will also be differences in trade-union membership, not to mention differences in the unions themselves (remember that the British Medical Association is a union). Social workers balance the demands employers and unions make with the professional decisions taken. Working closely with other professions imposes yet another set of demands and this same sort of balancing act is being performed by everyone.

A third useful skill is being able to do social work through someone else. Sometimes the GP may be very close to an old person, and may be a familiar and well-trusted figure. We need to be able to offer services through the GP. We might, for example, deal with a telephone application by explaining the criteria to the GP and getting her to feed the information from the client back to us. Sometimes a housing assistant is the only person who can gain entry to the flat of a confused elderly person, and social workers might have to assess the need for meals on wheels, or the need for a psychiatric referral through the housing assistant. Sometimes a home help can help to deal with a bereavement. Sharing skills is not easy, but from the point of view of the recipient it can be a way of offering help which would otherwise be unavailable.

Finally, some group-work skills are invaluable both for understanding what is going on in a group and in coping with inter-professional meetings. All the basic group-work knowledge outlined in the sensible and straightforward books by people like Michael Preston-Shoot (1987), applies to meetings. Take, for example, the knowledge that we have relating to group development. Although different theorists call the phases by different names, it is well known that most groups go through a period of preliminaries, when there is a lot of inconsequential talk, which is in fact a way for people to check each other out. This is followed by a period of task-centred activity which usually comes to an abrupt halt as the group hits a patch of turbulence and renegotiation. If this is accomplished, the group can then continue productively. This sort of knowledge is invaluable if we are trying to understand what is happening: we will not, for example, rush the preliminaries if we realise they are essential. Neither will we despair if the group suddenly seems to fall apart. We can use this upheaval if we understand it to rethink things like objectives or group norms.

In the same way, knowledge about things like leadership, style, scapegoating and homogeneity of membership can enhance an understanding of what is going on. This knowledge must make social workers more skilled in groups because it alerts us to the processes as well as to the content. The skills are more difficult to outline. Perhaps the most important is being ready and able to tackle the processes if we feel that they are becoming counter-productive. This can be done privately, when it might be pointed out to someone that she is, let us say, getting into a power struggle with another member, thus preventing the meeting getting on with its business. It can be done publicly, too. This is usually done as a joke, and the subsequent laughter enables people to absorb the information without loss of face. More usefully, some groups need occasionally to take time out to confront their tangled processes. This can be a brief ten minutes to discuss what is actually happening, or it may be useful to put processes on to the agenda for the next meeting. An example of the first would be a meeting about whether someone was to be labelled 'geriatric' or 'psychogeriatric'. Imagine two doctors locked into issues of status and power. It might be helpful to point this out, and suggest that a moment spent on criteria would be useful. An example of the second might be a team meeting that was apparently demoralised and irritable deciding to take the group itself as its next meeting's business.

Both these examples might seem terrifying, but a little practice is all that is required. Rehearsals are often useful and are a technique which I think could be more widely used. Get a group of social work colleagues to play the roles of the key people in the inter-professional team meeting, and then try out ways of pointing out to them what is going wrong. This can be done very gently – as if they were doing you a favour by sorting themselves out. Similarly, interventions like the second example only need to be broached and will often be taken up enthusiastically. Most people are aware of being bored, frustrated or upset by the processes of a group without really understanding why. Obviously an intervention of this sort will throw the group into turmoil and will deflect the group from its task, so it is not an intervention to be used too often.

It might, in some instances, be better to work through someone else. It is very often helpful for people who are very task-centred to have someone privately point out that Mike X is being scapegoated or that John A and Susan B are so absorbed in each other that they contribute nothing. There is a tricky problem of whether social workers have a mandate to interfere with what is going on. I think that we share an equal responsibility with everyone else to provide as good a service as possible. If facilitating the function of a group of professionals does this, then it will have been worthwhile. At the very least, the furniture can be moved to a more congenial lay-out!

There will, however, always be people who are quite awful to work with. This is a problem that needs dealing with in the same purposeful way that any other problem is dealt with. The first thing to do is to thoroughly analyse what is going on. Dr Q is arrogant and overbearing. Does she feel insecure, has she just learned bad behaviour from her mentors, or does she really feel that she knows best? Having properly identified the problem, you can either set about making her feel more secure, teaching her better manners or pointing out to her occasions when she does not know best. This may sound far-fetched but it certainly can work. A little extra attention and interest can reassure her that she is valued. Working out a system of reinforcing good behaviour and ignoring the bad can prove to be effective over time, but determination is required. Reminding her of occasions when she needs other people's knowledge and skill can be done very gently but firmly. Some social workers set about this enabling business automatically and in a kind way. Some seem unable to do it, perhaps because of the need to have a scapegoat. The skills required with difficult colleagues are no different from those used with an insecure, a cantankerous or a know-all old lady. This underlies the central theme of this section, which is that social workers have skills that are used to help clients that can be easily translated for use with professional colleagues.

6

New Ideas

In this last rather brief chapter I shall try to pull some threads together and talk about the directions that social work with elderly people can take. This is important because the potential demand for help will increase and social workers will be gradually consolidating the skills we have rather hurriedly learned. In this respect, perhaps, social workers should be self-conscious about our practice, and make every effort to evaluate it, however tentatively, and write it up for mutual benefit. The BASW Guidelines (Marshall, 1988) on dementia show how practitioners can share their very latest skills which are developing very fast in this area of work.

However, first some words on newness. There is a tendency in social work, as in any other profession, to regard innovatory practices *per se* as good. I suppose this is partly due to the evangelical enthusiasm of innovators, who must always invest a great deal of themselves in their efforts, and partly because in the field of social work with old people social workers are ready to grasp at anything which seems fresh and interesting, since much work is hard and unrewarding slog. It is almost like the fashion industry. Everyone is suddenly talking about and ready to try a particular new style, while those who ignore the trend are condemned for being out of date. In the mid-1980s, for example, in our field the main concern was respite for the helpers; in the late 1980s we are preoccupied with value for money. Academics are particularly notorious. Gauging what ideas are likely to make successful research applications is a skill all by itself. This does not mean that the ensuing research findings should be disregarded, though all too often they are. Sadly it seems that innovations in practice are very

108

seldom built on research evidence; they are much more likely
to be based on imitations of other practical projects in other
parts of the country – or even other parts of the world. A
well-written description in the Sunday newspapers or *Community Care* seems to be worth a hundred reports of research.

It is hard to see what factors collect to form a trend or
fashion in social work. Clearly in view of expenditure cuts any
new idea that saves money is more likely to get a hearing. At
the same time, trends must relate to other ideological develop-
ments. I have a feeling, for example, that, some fifteen years
behind town planners, social workers are beginning to discover a need to consult with clients and their communities.
Participation seems to be an emerging trend – time will tell
whether it really catches on. I give this as an illustration
without intending to criticise the principle. The point here is
that social workers are perhaps too ready to seize things that
are new without reflecting on the extent to which they have
been evaluated. So one of the aims of this chapter is to
consider some sort of balance between the dynamism and
enthusiasm that characterises new projects, and the experience and skill already existing in traditional social work
methods.

To digress for a moment, I want to consider the recipients
of social work skills. Throughout this book I hope I have
avoided the trap of generalising about elderly people. A fine
line has to be trod between seeing every single person as
unique and some groups as having problems in common. The
degree to which people generalise about '*the* elderly' is surprising, when you think that being 'elderly' can span thirty
years of someone's life and that elderly people are just as
varied in their characteristics as the rest of the population.
Making general remarks about all 35 year-olds would be
foolish enough, but to make sweeping statements about everyone between 35 and 65 would be idiotic. So somewhere in
between treating old people as unique individuals and 'the
elderly' is the proper position to be in, and exactly where will
depend on the problem. One way round this problem of
generalising is to ask old people themselves what they want.
Joan Cooper (1980) shows one way of doing this in her groups
of old people who did share one problem – imminent dis-

charge from hospital. She found some quite surprising views from her participants. One of the most interesting was that they wanted convenient and reasonable housing in mixed communities rather than in communities of old people.

An equally fine line has to be drawn between exciting innovation and thorough consolidation of existing practice. Most of this book has been about the extra skills required to work with old people, but of course basic social work skills are very appropriate.

At the moment most of the skills are best developed and evaluated in the help given to children and their families. What is needed is a translation of these skills to practice with old people. One example that springs to mind is that of Mrs Tennant, who was in hospital. She had been living with her spinster sister since she was widowed some fifteen years before. She was now in her late 70s and in hospital for diabetes and other related complications. Her sister did not want her back. She herself was arthritic and claimed that they had never really got on anyway, but they had coped while both were fit and able to pursue their own interests. Her son's wife disliked her so there was no possibility of a home there, besides the lack of space with three teenage children in the house. Her daughter was in Canada and her other sister lived in a one-bedroomed flat. Mrs Tennant needed a lot of counselling to help her come to terms with this rejection by her family. The social worker had to help her to review her relationships with each of them and to recognise the reasons for the apparent abandonment. Some of these reasons went back to her childhood, when she and her sisters were in an atmosphere of intense and painful rivalry for their mother's attention. This sort of counselling is no different from the help social workers give to children in care when no relative seems able or willing to help. The child has to make sense of the rejection in terms that are not damaging to her self-esteem. Without this adjustment being made, neither the child nor women like Mrs Tennant is going to settle in their present situation, or plan for a new kind of future.

Social workers can make this kind of translation of most of the skills offered to children and families. Family therapy, for example, can be most helpful in untangling the complex relationships in some families who have 'acting-out' grannies rather than 'acting-out' teenagers. It can be argued that many old people behave just like adolescents. Perhaps in part because they did not have the leisure in their youth. Behaviour modification programmes can help families and care staff with behaviour problems in their elderly relatives and residents, particularly where small instances of eccentric behaviour are causing distress to carers and others who share the home. There is ever-increasing evidence of the phenomenon of non-accidental injuries to old people, and all the skills practised on parents who injure their children should be perfectly appropriate for people who injure their elderly relatives. The problems are essentially the same.

Similarly, the skills offered to a group of parents of children in care or groups of the children themselves can be translated to groups of relatives of old people in old people's homes or groups of the old people themselves. Once again the problems are the same in essence. Similarly, advocacy skills are the same. Curiously, social workers interested in welfare rights have only recently devoted much time to elderly people, who are the major group of recipients of income support. Community development work with older people is very slowly emerging in practice: there is still too little about it in the literature.

It is in the area of indirect skills that most of the new efforts are being made. This is understandable considering that most indirect skills are about reorganising and generating resources. There is a very patchy collection of services for old people. Some provision has happened very quickly and with too little evaluation, like sheltered accommodation and volunteer visiting schemes. Other sorts of provision scarcely exist at all, such as special services for black and ethnic minority elderly people, or a proper range of types of accommodation or night-sitting schemes. It is therefore not surprising that the exciting area of innovation has been in this area of social work. Indeed, it is quite proper because what is urgently needed is a rich and varied pattern of services specially designed to meet the needs of elderly people.

What is needed, as with every client group, is a range of services and resources plus a set of skills to help people

individually with their personal problems. Let us take homeless elderly people as an example. Taking a broad view of
homelessness, homeless people exist in hospitals and hostels
for the homeless; they are inappropriately placed in long-term
nursing homes and residential care; they are living in houses
that are too big, too cold, too dangerous or too squalid. Some
of their problems could be solved if we put our minds to
generating new kinds of accommodation. We need to consider
shared tenancies, or small blocks of flats for people with
particular problems. Influence could be exerted to get some
accommodation converted, insulated or adapted to be more
convenient. We could invest some effort into tenancy selection
procedures in housing associations and the local authority to
make sure that the people who can adjust to and really need
sheltered accommodation are the people who get it. Some of
these indirect skills would be new to some social workers, but
they can be every bit as rewarding as the direct skills. Direct
skills, too, are needed in work with homeless people. Skills like
helping them to adjust to new environments, like helping
people gain confidence in their abilities and helping them
learn how to cope in their new homes are all required. Sometimes people need help in relinquishing their former way of life
and trying a new one. Helpers, volunteers and support have to
be organised. The mixture is some old, some new; old people
need the whole lot.

In conclusion I want to look at some of the qualities that I
think should characterise social work help in the rest of this
century, help that will inevitably focus on the older old people,
whose numbers will increase proportionally and whose need
for help no social work agency will be able to completely
avoid.

First, a characteristic of the help must be that it is firmly set
in a inter-disciplinary context. It would be disastrous if social
workers became isolated in our efforts because the problems of
old old people never neatly fall into any one profession's terms
of reference. Professional demarcation is not helpful to any
client group, but it is least helpful to a group whose problems
are such an inextricable tangle of health, housing, finances,
morale, families, and so on. Social workers have to be able to
work alongside other professionals and we have to be in the

business of breaking down boundaries. At one level this is about participating in any reorganisation of organisations such as the National Health Service, social services/work departments, etc., and at the other extreme it is about jobs like working with the district nurse to persuade someone to accept treatment for a leg ulcer.

A second characteristic of the help provided must be a willingness to support, train, mobilise and share care with a host of non-professional people. I do not want to collude with the current and often quite foolhardy policies for community care, where politicians of every party seek simply to off-load their responsibilities onto exhausted, demoralised and sometimes threadbare communities. Nevertheless, social workers are in the business of helping the helpers, whoever they might be.

This brings me to a third point, which is that old people should be asked what they want. A major justification for community care must be that many old people want to remain outside institutions if at all possible. Asking people what they want in a way that gives them genuine choice would enable services to be made more sensitive to their needs. Choice is a concept many professionals find difficult to practice beyond the choice between accepting or rejecting a service. We are so used to seeing ourselves as experts.

Fourth, I think that help has to be geared to encouraging more older people themselves to make a contribution to society. The vast potential of skills, experience and time that older people have to offer, given the opportunity is largely neglected. This is an important way of combating the ageist notion that old old people are simply a burden.

And finally, I think social work with old people has got to be enjoyable. It can be challenging, stimulating, rewarding and fun. We should make every effort to see that it is all of these.

Appendices

I

Discharge from Hospital – an Assessment List

This is a list of points to consider when organising the discharge of an old person from hospital. It was originally formulated by the Continuing Care Project (1975) which tested it and found it helpful. It has been updated.

Section I

1. Name ....

2. Address ....

   ....

3. Hospital .... Ward ....

4. Consultant ....

5. Date of admission ....

6. Date form completed ....

7. Date of birth ....

8. Next of kin ....

   Relationship ....

   Address ....

   ....

9. Religion ....

10. GP's name ....

    Address ....

    ....

116

Section II

11. Patient

    lives alone

         "   with spouse who will be able to cope

         "   "   "   "   " require more help

         "   "   relative who will be able to cope

         "   "   "   "   " require more help

         "   "   friend who will be able to cope

         "   "   "   "   " require more help

    Other arrangements ....

    ....

12. Other help available from   relative

                               neigbours

                               friends

                               other

                               none

13. This help available   full

                        night time only

                        daytime only

                        irregular

                        none

14. Person providing extra help

                      will be able to cope

                would appreciate further help

15.   Accommodation   House

                                            Flat

                          Sheltered housing

                          Residential home

                             Nursing home

                                           Other

Specify ....

16.   Ownership   Self

                                         Council

                          Private landlord

                                          Other

Specify ....

Do you have housing benefit?   Yes/No

17.   Facilities

Hot water supply   Yes/No

Unavoidable stairs or steps   Inside

                                        Outside

                                           None

Toilet   Upstairs

                                     Downstairs

                                        Outside

Bedroom   Upstairs

                                     Downstairs

Heating   Adequate

                                    Inadequate

Telephone   Own

Within reach

No access

Alarm system – details ....

18.   Income   Old age pension

Income support

Attendance allowance

Occupational pension

Full employment

Part-time employment

19.   Services already received

Health visitor

District nurse

Home help

Meals on wheels

Old People's Club

Church/voluntary contacts

Bus pass

Social worker

Other, specify ....

None

20.   Previous admission to hospital

None

Over 6 months ago

Within last 6 months

Within last fortnight

21.   How are you going to get home from hospital?

....

Extra information on domestic situation which will not fit into above sections

....

....

....

Section III – Brief medical details

22.   Diagnosis if possible ....

....

(otherwise use boxes below)

Medical:	Chest	Orthopaedic:	U. Limb
	Heart		L. Limb
	CNS		Spine
	GIT		Other
	Other		
Surgical:	Abdominal	Chest	Other

23.   Prognosis   Full recovery

Partial recovery

No recovery

24.   Relevant medical background

Previous severe injury

"   "   medical illness

"   "   surgical illness

Nothing known

25. Present mental condition

                      Alert   Mild confusion

              Unco-operative   Violent

26. Estimated date of discharge

27. Extra information on medical details ....

....

....,..............

Section IV – Patient's likely condition on discharge

28. Mobility   Patient will be:

                    Fully mobile including stairs

                    Fully mobile excluding stairs

                    Able to walk length of ward

                    In need of assistance/aids

                    Chairfast or bedfast

29. Self-care.   Patient will be:

                    Able to feed herself

                    In need of help

                    Unable to feed herself

                    Able to dress herself

                    In need of help

                    Unable to dress herself

                    Able to wash herself

                    In need of help

                    Unable to wash herself

30. Eyesight   Good   31. Hearing   Good

                 Fair   Fair

                 Bad   Bad

32. Continence. Patient will be: Fully continent

                                  Occasionally incontinent

                                  Incontinent of urine

                                  Doubly incontinent

Extra information on patient's condition ....

....

....

II

Useful Addresses

Carers National Association
29 Chilworth Mews
London W2 3RG
(Tel: 01 724 7776)

Alzheimers Disease Society
158/160 Balham High Road
London SW12 9BN
(Tel: 01 675 6557)

Alzheimers Scotland
33 Castle Street
Edinburgh EH2 3DN
(Tel: 031 220 4886)

Age Concern England
Bernard Sunley House
60 Pitcairn Road
Mitcham
Surrey CR4 3LL
(Tel: 01 640 5431)

Age Concern Wales
4th Floor
1 Cathedral Road
Cardiff CF1 9SD
(Tel: 0222 371566)

Age Concern Northern Ireland
6 Lower Crescent
Belfast BT7 1NR
(Tel: 0232 245729)

Age Concern Scotland
54a Fountainbridge
Edinburgh EH3 9PT
(Tel: 031 228 5656)

British Association for Service to the Elderly
119 Hassell Street

Newcastle-under-Lyme
Staffs ST5 1AX
(Tel: 0782 661033)

British Association of Social Workers
16 Kent Street
Birmingham B5 6RD
(Tel: 021 622 3911)

Centre for Policy on Ageing
25 – 31 Ironmonger Row
London EC1U 3PQ
(Tel: 01 253 1787)

Help the Aged
16 St James Walk
London EC1R OBE
(Tel: 01 253 0253)

Scottish Action on Dementia
c/o Alzheimers Scotland
33 Castle Street
Edinburgh EH2 3DN
(Tel: 031 220 4886)

Strathclyde Elderly Forum
Unit E6, Block 6
Templeton Business Centre
60 Templeton Street
Glasgow G40 1DA
(Tel: 041 551 0595)

For material for those working with groups of dementing people:

The Winslow Press
Telford Road
Bicester
Oxon OX6 OTS
(Tel: 0869 244644)

III

The Mental Health Act 1983

This Act deals with the compulsory admission of people to psychiatric hospitals. The sections under which this is done are as follows.

Section 2

Under this section a patient is admitted for observation and treatment for up to 28 days if:

1. She is suffering from mental impairment or severe mental impairment of a nature or degree which warrants detention.
2. She ought to be detained in the interests of her own health and safety or with a view to the protection of other persons.

Two doctors and an approved social worker have to sign this.

Section 3

Under this section a patient is admitted for treatment for up to six months. This can only be written after a care plan has been formulated. It must be signed by two doctors who have to give their reasons. Patients can be discharged while still under this section, and can be readmitted without the need for a fresh section.

Section 4

This section is used to admit people in an emergency. It only lasts for three days and is for observation. It only needs one doctor to sign it.

Note: Section 12 specifies that the approved social worker is exhorted to search for every alternative other than a compulsory admission. If a nearest relative signs a section then the approved social worker has to provide a social welfare report. If the nearest relative does not sign then the social worker has to show she has made every effort to consult. If either of the two doctors is not known to the relative then the social worker has to explain why.

125

IV

The Mental Health (Scotland) Act 1984

This Act deals with the compulsory admission of people to psychiatric hospitals. The sections under which this is done are:

Section 18. Under this section the patient is admitted for six months then reviewed requires two medical recommendations: one normally the GP. Application made by either the nearest relative or a mental health officer, addressed to the managers of the hospital must be approved by the sheriff. The application should include the Mental Health Officer's opinion as to whether the application should be granted and a statement of the grounds on which that opinion is based. When the application has been approved by the Sherrif it is the duty of the managers of the hospital to notify the Mental Welfare Commission.

Section 24. This is an 'emergency' recommendation stating that by reasons of mental disorder it is urgently necessary for the person's health or safety or for the protection of other people, that he should be admitted to a hospital. This lasts for three days. It can be made by a medical practitioner.

Section 26. This section relates to short-term detention and often follows a Section 24. Consent to continued detention must be obtained from the nearest relative or by a Mental Health Officer. It lasts for 28 days.

V

The Mental Health (Northern Ireland) Order 1986

The compulsory admission of people to psychiatric hospitals in Northern Ireland.

Part 2 Article 4

All patients compulsorily admitted to hospital will be held initially for a period of assessment of up to 14 days before being admitted for treatment. The application is made on the grounds

(a) that the applicant 'is suffering from mental disorder of a nature or degree which warrants his detention in hospital for assessment (or for assessment followed by medical treatment)', *and*
(b) failure to so detain 'would create a substantial likelihood of serious physical harm to himself or to other persons'.

The period of assessment is to give time for thorough assessment and for clearly establishing the need for treatment before a period of longer detention is entered into.

The application for assessment is made either by the nearest relative or by an approval social worker.

The applicant must use prescribed forms and to have seen the patient within the previous two days. It has to be accompanied by a medical recommendation.

When social workers are making the application they must take all possible steps to consult the nearest relative and if they object then the social worker must consult another approved social worker. If after this consultation he is satisfied, the application may proceed, provided the nearest relative's objections are recorded on the application form.

If the application for assessment has been made by the nearest relative a social worker may not be involved at that stage.

Article 5(6) then requires a social worker, not necessarily an approved social worker, to interview the patient and provide the responsible medical officer with a social circumstances report.

It must cover all possible options, consult relevant professional and other people and be completed as soon as practicable in order to be available as early as possible in the assessment period.

Article 10

Article 10 is unique to Northern Ireland. 'It enables any periods for which a patient has been detained for assessment and which have not been immediately followed by a period of detention for treatment to be disregarded, for certain purposes, i.e. treated as if they had never occured.'

There are a few specific exceptions to this provision but generally it is meant to help safeguard people's rights to employment etc. without prejudice.

Article 12 – Detention for Treatment

'During the second 7 days of the assessment period the patient must be examined by a Part II doctor to decide whether it is necessary to detain for treatment beyond that period.' The doctor has to be satisfied that the patient should be further detained on the grounds:

1. that he is suffering from mental illness or some mental impairment,
2. that he is likely to cause severe physical harm to himself or others, and
3. that no other methods of dealing with the patient are available or appropriate
4. a report must be furnished on a prescribed form (10).

The patient may then be detained for 6 months dating from the admission date.

This order can be renewed after the first 6 months for a further 6 months and thereafter for a year at a time.

VI

Section 47 of the National Assistance Act 1948

The National Assistance Act and its 1951 amendment is generally used for old people who are living in squalid and hazardous circumstances. The grounds for its use are given here:

1. The following provisions of this Section shall have effect for the purposes of securing the necessary care and attention for persons who

   (a) are suffering from grave chronic disease *or*, being aged, infirm *or* physically incapacitated, are living in insanitary conditions, *and*
   (b) are unable to devote to themselves, are not receiving from other persons, proper care and attention.

2. If the Medical Officer of Health certifies in writing to the appropriate authority that he is satisfied after thorough enquiry and consideration that the interests of any such person as aforesaid residing in the area of the authority, or for preventing injury to the health of, or serious nuisance to, other persons, it is necessary to remove any such person as aforesaid from the premises in which he is residing, the appropriate authority may apply to a court of summary jurisdiction having jurisdiction in the place where the premises are situated for an Order under the next following sub-section.

In less legal terms a person must be ill *or* old, living in insanitary conditions, *and* inadequately cared for. Removal must also be in the old person's interests or must prevent serious harm to her health or serious nuisance to other people.

Application is made to the court, and providing that some establishment agrees to admit the person she can be detained there for up to three months. The person has to be given a week's notice that this will happen. In 1951 the section was amended. Under the amendment, application can be made to a JP and removal can occur immediately provided that two doctors (one of whom is the community physician) sign the papers. This order lasts for up to three weeks.

References

References in this book have been kept to an absolute minimum so this list must not be seen as comprehensive in any way. Nevertheless, included in this list are many books and articles that I think social workers working with old people ought to read. The six texts I consider most useful for social workers are marked with an asterisk (*).

Abrams, M. (1978) *Beyond Three Score Years and Ten*, Mitcham, Age Concern.

*Age Concern, *Your Rights*, Mitcham, Age Concern.

*Age Concern England (1986) *The Law and Vulnerable Elderly People*, Mitcham, Age Concern England.

Balint, M. (1957) *The Doctor, His Patient, and the Illness*, London, Pitman.

Bland, R. (1987) *Is It For Me?*, HMSO, Edinburgh.

Brittain, V. (1933) *Testament of Youth*, London, Victor Gollancz.

Brittain, V. (1957) *Testament of Experience*, London, Victor Gollancz.

Burley L.E., Currie, C.T., Smith, R.G. and Williamson, J. (1979) 'Contribution From Geriatric Medicine within Acute Medical Wards', *British Medical Journal*, 2, pp. 90–92.

Butler, A., Oldman, C., Greve, J., (1983) *Sheltered Housing for the elderly*, London, Allen & Unwin.

Caplan, G. (1964) *Principles of preventative Psychiatry*, New York, Basic Books.

Central Statistical Office (1974) *Social Trends*, London, HMSO.

Challis, D. and Davies, B. (1980) 'A new approach to community care for the elderly', *British Journal of Social Work*, X, 1, Spring, pp. 1–18.

Continuing Care Project (1975) *Going Home*, Liverpool (now 20 Westfield Road, Edgbaston, Birmingham).

Cooper, J.D. (1980) *Social Groupwork with Elderly People in Hospital*, London, Beth Johnson Foundation.

Coulshed, V. (1980) 'A unitary approach to the care of the hospitalised elderly mentally ill', *British Journal of Social Work*, 10, 1, Spring, pp. 19–33.

Evans, G., Hughes, B., Wilkin, D. and Jolley, D. (1981) 'The management of mental and physical impairment in non-specialist residential homes for the elderly', Research Report No. 4, University Hospital of South Manchester Psychogeriatric Unit, Research Section.

Forster, D.P. and Tiplady, P. (1980) 'Doctors and compulsory procedures:

section 47 of the National Assistance Act, 1948', *British Medical Journal*, 8 March, p. 739.

Gilmore, M., Bruce, N. and Hunt, M. (1974) *The Work of the Nursing Team in General Practice*, London, Council for Education and Training of Health Visitors.

Glendinning F. and Pearson M. (1988) *The Black and Ethnic Minority Elders in Britain: Health Needs and Access to Services*, Keele, Health Education Authority and Department of Adult and Continuing Education, University of Keele.

Goldberg, E.M. and Warburton, R.W. (1979) *Ends and Means in Social Work*, National Institute for Social Work, London, Allen & Unwin.

Griffiths, Sir Roy, (1988) *Community Care: Agenda For Action*, London, HMSO.

Hewins, A. (ed.) (1981) *The Dillen: Memories of a Man of Stratford-upon-Avon*, London, Elm Tree Books.

Hey, A. (1979) 'Organising teams – alternative patterns', in M. Marshall, M. Preston-Shoot, and E. Wincott (eds), *Teamwork: For and Against*, Birmingham, BASW Publication.

Hunt, A. (1978) *The Elderly at Home*, London, Office of Population Censuses and Surveys, HMSO.

*Marris, P. (1974) *Loss and Change*, London, Routledge & Kegan Paul.

Marshall, M. and Newton, S. (1981) 'Learning lessons from work with the elderly'. *Social Work Today*, 12, 20, 20 January.

*Marshall, M. (ed.) (1988) *Guidelines for Social Workers working with People with Dementia and their Carers* Birmingham, BASW.

Melling, C., Crawford, A., Wilkieson, S. (1986) 'Pensioner Power' *Community Action*, June/July.

Middleton, L. (1988) *So much for So Few: A View of Sheltered Accomodation*, Liverpool Institute of Human Ageing.

Midwinter E. and Tester S. (1987) *Polls Apart? Older Voters and the 1987 General Election* London, Centre for Policy on Ageing.

Murphy E. (1986) *Dementia and Mental Illness in the Old*, London, Papermac.

Naylor, G. and Hardwood, E. (1975) 'Old dogs, new tricks: age and ability', *Psychology Today*, 1, April.

Newton, S. (1979) 'A story of a white lamb and a quiet, deaf old lady', *Social Work Today*, 11 (15), 11 February.

Norman, A. (1987) *Rights and Risk*, London, Centre for Policy on Ageing, (second reprint with revised foreword, first printed 1980).

Norman, A. (1985) *Triple Jeopardy: Growing Old in a Second Homeland*, London, Centre for Policy on Ageing.

Office of Population Censuses and Surveys (1987) *Population Projections 1985–2025*, London, HMSO.

Parad, H.J. (1966) 'The use of time-limited crisis intervention in community mental health programming', *Social Services Review*, 40, September, pp. 275–82.

Parkes, C.M. (1975) *Bereavement: Studies of Grief in Adult Life*, Harmondsworth, Penguin.

Patti, R.J. and Resnick, H. (1975) 'Changing the agency from within', in

B.R. Compton and B. Galway (eds), *Social Work Processes*, Homewood, III., Dorsey Press.

Payne, M. (1982) *Working in Teams*, London, Macmillan.

Phillipson, C. (1982) *Capitalism and the Construction of Old Age*, London, Macmillan.

Preston-Shoot M. (1987) *Effective Groupwork*, London, Macmillan.

Rapoport, L. (1962) 'The state of crisis: some theoretical considerations', *Social Services Review*, 36, June, pp. 211–17.

*Rowlings, C. (1981) *Social Work with Elderly People*, London, Allen & Unwin.

Royal College of Psychiatrists and British Geriatric Society, (1978) *Guidelines for Collaboration between Geriatric Physicians and Psychiatrists in the Care of the Elderly*, Document No. EFCC 16/78 (ii)C 27/78, 19 January.

Sachs, V.K. (1968) 'Crisis intervention', *Public Welfare*, 26, April, pp. 112–17.

*Scottish Action on Dementia (1988) *Dementia and the Law: the Challenge Ahead*, Edinburgh.

Smith, C.R. (1982) *Social Work with the Dying and Bereaved*, London, Macmillan.

Thompson, T. (1981) *Edwardian Childhoods*, London, Routledge & Kegan Paul.

Tinker, A. (1984) *The Elderly in Modern Society*, (2nd edn) London, Longman.

Wilson, A. (1978) *Finding a Voice: Asian Women in Britain*, London, Virago.

Index

133